<u>AUTHOR'S NOTE</u>

Hello Readers!!

I wish to extend my sincere thanks for choosing this book and showing interest in understanding Micro Small & Medium Enterprises.

The inspiration for this book came from my own experiences with loss and the passage of time. Like many of us, I have wondered about the ripple effects of the decisions we make each day, no matter how small they seem at the time. In the wake of a personal tragedy, I found myself questioning how my actions, or even my inactions, might have influenced the paths of those around me.

In my years of experience as a Banker, I've worked with individuals from all walks of life; executives, entrepreneurs, and young professionals; all with varying degrees of financial knowledge. Despite these differences, one thing was consistent; most people don't feel they have the financial tools or mindset to confidently navigate. Too often, they feel overwhelmed by conflicting advice, economic uncertainty, and the sheer complexity of financial products. This book is my attempt to give readers a clear, step-by-step roadmap to a successful entrepreneurial journey.

Financial freedom isn't just about accumulating wealth, it's about having the confidence to make informed decisions, the discipline to stick to your plan, and the awareness to adjust when necessary.

This book is intended for all those who wish to start their own entrepreneurship journey and are looking for supportive guidance as to how, where, when and what to start.

I am sure that this book will also be beneficial for all those who are appearing for any interview or competitive exams.

I would miss it if I did not express my deepest gratitude to my banker colleagues for their unwavering support throughout this process. whose meticulous eyes and feedback helped ensure that this book was as accessible and engaging as it could be.

ABHIK MITRA

TABLE OF CONTENT

PREFACE

The evolution of Micro, Small, and Medium Enterprises (MSMEs) in India reflects a dynamic journey marked by policy shifts, economic changes, and increasing recognition of their role in the economy. Here's an overview of the key phases in the evolution of MSMEs in India: -

- Before independence, small-scale industries in India were predominantly artisanal and localized. These included traditional crafts, textiles, and small-scale manufacturing. The focus was on industrialization and building a self-reliant economy. Early policies were geared towards large-scale industries, with MSMEs being relatively neglected.

- The first major recognition of MSMEs came with the establishment of the Small-Scale Industries (SSI) sector in the 1960s. The government began to introduce policies to promote these enterprises, including incentives and support. The Industrial Policy Resolution of 1980 further highlighted the importance of the SSI sector in economic development. The policy aimed to support MSMEs through subsidies, financial support, and preferential treatment in procurement.

- The 1991 economic reforms marked a shift towards a market-oriented economy. The liberalization of the Indian economy led to increased competition, impacting MSMEs which had to adapt to a more competitive environment. The early 2000s saw a more structured approach to MSME development. The **Micro, Small and Medium Enterprises Development (MSMED) Act, 2006** was a significant milestone, providing a legal framework for the growth and regulation of MSMEs. Initiatives such as the National Manufacturing Competitiveness Programme (NMCP) and the **Credit Guarantee Fund Scheme** were introduced to enhance the competitiveness and financial stability of MSMEs.

- **Startup India Initiative**, launched in 2016, this initiative aimed to provide support for new ventures and foster innovation among MSMEs. The government introduced several relief measures, including the **Atmanirbhar Bharat Abhiyan**, which included financial packages, loans, and other support mechanisms for MSMEs.

- Startup India Initiative, launched in 2016, this initiative aimed to provide support for new ventures and foster innovation among MSMEs. The government introduced several relief measures, including the Atmanirbhar Bharat Abhiyan, which included financial packages, loans, and other support mechanisms for MSMEs.

- The promotion of Micro, Small, and Medium Enterprises (MSMEs) serves several important purposes:

  1. Economic Growth: MSMEs contribute significantly to national economic development by generating employment, fostering innovation, and driving local and regional economic growth.
  2. Job Creation: MSMEs are major employers, particularly in developing regions, helping to reduce unemployment and underemployment by providing diverse job opportunities.
  3. Diversification: They contribute to economic diversification by operating in various sectors and markets, which can make economies more resilient to shocks.
  4. Innovation and Competitiveness: MSMEs often drive innovation by bringing new products, services, and business models to market. Their presence can also stimulate competition, benefiting consumers through improved products and services.
  5. Local Development: By operating in local and rural areas, MSMEs contribute to regional development and reduce economic disparities between urban and rural regions.
  6. Support for Larger Enterprises: MSMEs often act as suppliers or partners to larger companies, helping to build robust supply chains and support the broader business ecosystem.
  7. Entrepreneurship Encouragement: Promoting MSMEs supports entrepreneurship by creating an environment where new businesses can start and thrive, fostering a culture of innovation and self-reliance.
  8. Resource Utilization: MSMEs often utilize local resources and skills, maximizing the use of available resources and contributing to sustainable development.

Overall, promoting MSMEs helps to build a more dynamic and resilient economy that benefits from a broad base of small and medium-sized enterprises.

Several countries have experienced significant economic development due to the robust growth and support of Micro, Small, and Medium Enterprises (MSMEs). Here are a few notable examples:

- Germany: Known for its "**Mittel stand**" sector, Germany's economy has been heavily influenced by its small and medium-sized enterprises. These firms are characterized by their strong regional focus, innovation, and high levels of specialization. The Mittel stand companies are crucial in driving Germany's export-led growth and have contributed to its reputation as an economic powerhouse in Europe.
- South Korea: South Korea's economic development has been greatly supported by its vibrant MSME sector. The government has provided substantial support through various policies and programs that promote innovation and technology in small businesses. MSMEs have played a key role in the country's rapid industrialization and export growth.
- India: India has seen significant economic contributions from its MSME sector, which represents a substantial portion of its GDP and employment. The sector includes a diverse range of industries, from manufacturing to services, and has been a vital component of the country's economic development and poverty reduction efforts. Government initiatives, such as easier access to credit and support for technology adoption, have further fuelled this growth.

- Taiwan: Taiwan's economy has been significantly bolstered by its small and medium-sized enterprises, particularly in the technology and manufacturing sectors. MSMEs in Taiwan have been instrumental in driving innovation, especially in high-tech industries, and have contributed to the country's reputation as a global technology hub. 

- Italy: Italy's economic landscape includes a strong MSME sector, especially in regions like Tuscany and Lombardy. These enterprises, often family-owned, are crucial in sectors such as fashion, automotive, and machinery. The diversity and innovation within Italy's MSME sector contribute to its economic dynamism and global competitiveness.

- Brazil: Brazil's MSME sector plays a crucial role in its economy, providing employment and contributing to regional development. The government's focus on supporting small businesses through various programs has helped in fostering economic growth and innovation.

These examples illustrate how MSMEs can be pivotal in driving economic development, innovation, and job creation, contributing significantly to the overall prosperity and stability of a country.

CHAPTER-1
PRE-REQUISITE FOR AN ENTREPRENEUR

Entrepreneurship and innovation can be considered fundamental aspects of human nature, though they may manifest differently across individuals and cultures. These tendencies are often seen as integral to human progress and survival, stemming from our ability to adapt to changing environments and solve complex problems.

Humans are innately curious and driven to understand the world around them. Innovation is the product of this curiosity; whether it's figuring out how to start a fire, inventing the wheel, or creating the internet. Our ability to think abstractly and conceptually allows us to innovate across a wide range of domains, from technology to social organization.

Innovation doesn't just happen once; it's a continuous process of refining existing ideas, processes, and products to make them more effective. The drive to improve the tools and systems we use is deeply embedded in human culture, from the earliest innovations in stone tools to today's advances.

Entrepreneurship and innovation often go hand in hand. Entrepreneurs are the ones who take innovations and turn them into practical, scalable businesses. Innovation without entrepreneurship can remain theoretical, while entrepreneurship without innovation can lead to mere replication rather than advancement.

Peter Drucker says that "The best way to predict the future is to create it. Entrepreneurship is neither a science nor an art. It is a practice."

Albert Schweitzer says that "Success is not the key to happiness. Happiness is the key to success. If you love what you are doing, you will be successful."

Becoming a successful micro or small entrepreneur involves several key prerequisites and qualities. Here are some essential factors to consider:
- <u>Business Idea and Planning:</u>
  1. *Innovative Idea*: A unique and viable business idea that addresses a market need or problem.
  2. *Business Plan*: A comprehensive plan outlining your business goals, target market, competition, marketing strategy, and financial projections.

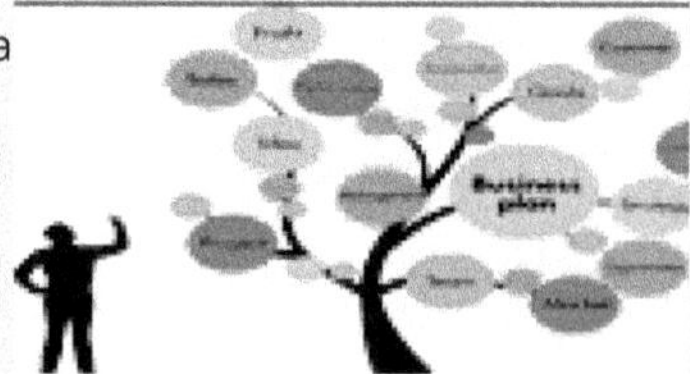

- <u>Knowledge and Skills:</u>
  1. *Industry Knowledge*: Understanding of the industry you're entering, including trends, challenges, and opportunities.
  2. *Entrepreneurial Skills*: Skills in areas such as marketing, sales, finance, and operations.

- Financial Management:
  1. *Initial Capital*: Sufficient funding to cover startup costs and initial operational expenses.
  2. *Financial Literacy*: Ability to manage finances, including budgeting, accounting, and understanding financial statements.

- Market Research and Strategy:
  1. *Market Understanding*: Knowledge of your target market, customer needs, and competitive landscape.
  2. *Marketing Strategy*: A clear strategy for reaching and attracting your target customers.

- Legal and Regulatory Compliance:
  1. *Business Registration*: Proper registration of your business according to local laws and regulations.
  2. *Permits and Licenses*: Necessary permits and licenses required for operating your business.

- Networking and Support:
  1. *Mentorship:* Guidance from experienced entrepreneurs or business mentors.
  2. *Networking:* Building connections with other business owners, suppliers, and potential customers.

- Resilience and Adaptability:
  1. *Problem-Solving Skills*: Ability to address and overcome challenges and setbacks.
  2. *Adaptability*: Flexibility to adjust your business strategy in response to changing market conditions or feedback.

- Customer Focus:
  1. *Customer Service*: Commitment to providing excellent customer service and building strong customer relationships.
  2. *Feedback Utilization*: Using customer feedback to improve products or services.

- Technology and Innovation:
  1. *Tech Savvy*: Understanding and utilizing relevant technology to enhance business operations and competitiveness.
  2. *Innovation*: Continuously seeking ways to improve and innovate within your business.

- Work Ethic and Commitment:
  1. *Dedication*: Willingness to invest time and effort into your business.
  2. *Persistence*: Ability to stay motivated and persistent despite challenges.

Success as a micro or small entrepreneur often depends on a combination of these factors, along with a strong passion for your business and a clear vision of what you want to achieve.

CHAPTER-2
SELECTION OF ACTIVITY

Selecting an activity for an enterprise for either starting a new business or deciding on the focus of an existing business, requires careful analysis and strategic decision-making. The activity chosen will define the direction of the business, influence its resources, and determine its efficiency for growth and sustainability. Here's a step-by-step guide to help select an appropriate activity for an enterprise:

- **Identify Your Interests and Expertise**: Start by considering what you are passionate about. An enterprise activity that aligns with your personal interests and expertise is more likely to keep you motivated and committed. Passion often translates into long-term perseverance, which is essential for the success of an enterprise. Assess your own professional skills, education, and experiences. What are you particularly good at? Choosing an activity that leverages your strengths will give you a competitive edge, allowing you to offer valuable products or services.

- **Conduct Market Research**: Research potential markets and industries to identify opportunities. Look for areas where there is demand for products or services that are currently under-served or have potential for improvement. Consider conducting surveys, interviews, or focus groups to understand the needs of your target audience. Pay attention to emerging market trends, economic shifts, and technological advancements. Industries such as health and wellness, sustainability, e-commerce, and technology often experience rapid growth, offering fresh opportunities for new ventures. Study competitors in the potential activity area. Understand their strengths and weaknesses and identify gaps in the market. What can you do differently or better. This analysis will help you position your enterprise in a way that capitalizes on unmet needs.

- **Evaluate Market Fit and Demand**: An enterprise is most successful when it solves a real problem or fulfils a specific need. Focus on activities that address clear pain points for your target customers. Whether it's improving efficiency, providing a better experience, or offering a unique solution, ensure there is a clear value proposition. Consider whether the activity is scalable. Can the business grow over time, and can it handle increasing demand. Scalability ensures that the business can expand without being overly burdened by resources or operational costs.

- **Assess Financial Viability**: Different activities require different levels of investment. Consider both the initial startup costs and the ongoing operational expenses. Some enterprises may require significant capital for inventory, technology, or infrastructure, while others may be more capital-light (e.g., service-based businesses). Analyse the potential for revenue generation in the chosen activity. Look at pricing models, margins, and sales forecasts. Be realistic about how long it might take to become profitable and what the income stream will look like over time. Estimate the profitability of the chosen activity by calculating the expected costs versus revenues. Evaluate whether the financial returns justify the investment of time, energy, and resources. Will the business be able to generate enough profit to sustain itself and grow.

- **Consider Legal and Regulatory Aspects**: Some activities are heavily regulated, such as healthcare, finance, or education. Ensure that you understand the legal and regulatory requirements for the industry you are considering, including licenses, permits, taxes, and compliance standards. Assess the risks associated with the activity. Some industries, such as technology or manufacturing, may involve higher financial or legal risks, while others may face competitive pressures. Understanding potential risks can help you develop strategies to mitigate them.

- **Analyse the Potential for Innovation**: Even in mature industries, there's often room for innovation. Think about how you can improve existing products, introduce new technologies, or offer a unique customer experience. Differentiation is key to standing out in competitive markets. Is there an opportunity to leverage technology in your activity. Technology can enhance operational efficiency, improve customer engagement, or streamline delivery. Consider how you can incorporate modern technologies such as AI, automation, or digital platforms to gain a competitive advantage. Test and Validate the Idea: Before fully committing to an activity, try to test your idea in a smaller, controlled environment. You can create a prototype, pilot your service, or run a minimum viable product (MVP) to gauge customer response and adjust your offering based on feedback. Engage with potential customers through beta testing, focus groups, or direct conversations. Their feedback will provide invaluable insights into whether the activity truly solves a need and is appealing to the target market. Be prepared to iterate on your idea. Rarely does a new business succeed without refining the product or service based on initial feedback. Flexibility and adaptability are key traits of successful entrepreneurs.

- **Alignment with Long-Term Goals**: Ensure that the activity you choose aligns with your personal or organizational mission and values. A business that is aligned with your vision is more likely to inspire you and those around you to stay committed in the long term. Consider the long-term horizon for your enterprise. Do you plan to scale and sell it, build it for passive income, or create a legacy brand? Choose an activity that fits your desired exit strategy or long-term business goals. Consider the Impact on Society and the Environment: Today's consumers are increasingly concerned about sustainability, ethics, and the social responsibility of businesses. Consider how your chosen activity can make a positive impact on society or the environment. Businesses that align with social causes or that implement sustainable practices often resonate more deeply with customers. As part of your selection process, think about how your enterprise can give back to the community or contribute to meaningful causes. A business with strong CSR initiatives often builds loyalty and a positive reputation. Selecting an activity for your enterprise is not just about identifying what seems like a profitable idea; it's about aligning your passions, expertise, market demand, and financial goals. By conducting thorough research, evaluating the viability of the idea, testing it with real customers, and ensuring it aligns with your long-term vision, you can choose an enterprise activity that has both business potential and personal fulfilment.

CHAPTER-3
CONSTITUTION OF BUSINESS

An entrepreneur interested in setting up a business venture must comply with several essential requirements and take important decision relating to which form of business constitution would embrace and with what effects and for how long on the journey to progress for the growth of enterprise. Choosing the right form of business organization depends on factors like the number of owners, liability preferences, capital requirements, governance structure, and long-term goals. Entrepreneurs in India can choose from a variety of options, each suited to different needs. While simpler forms like sole proprietorships or partnerships offer more flexibility and fewer regulatory requirements, structures like private limited companies and LLPs provide greater protection from liabilities, making them more suitable for larger or growing businesses.

In India, there are several forms of business organizations, each with its own legal structure, benefits, and challenges. The main types of business organizations in India are as follows:

- **Sole Proprietorship**

  Advantages-

  1. In sole proprietorship constitution the business activity is owned by a single Individual who enjoys the 100% profit earned by the enterprise. The proprietor is equally liable for the losses and liabilities incurred by the organisation. This form of organisation is suitable for small businesses units where business complexities are extremely limited.
  2. No formal registration is required in this constitution, except for tax purposes. One can register under the Goods and Services Tax (GST) if turnover exceeds the prescribed threshold.
  3. The proprietor has an obligation to unlimited liability (personal assets are at risk if the business fails).
  4. Easy and inexpensive to set up. No need for formal agreements or regulatory compliance beyond taxation. Taxation is simpler, with income taxed under the personal income tax regime. Flexible structure and easy to dissolve.

  Disadvantages-

  1. Unlimited personal liability.
  2. Limited access to capital and financing options.
  3. Limited growth potential due to reliance on a single individual for management and operations.
  4. Business continuity issues if the owner dies or becomes incapacitated.

  Documents required to form a Sole proprietorship enterprise-

  1. KYC document of proprietor
  2. Registration under Shop & Establishment act.
  3. GST registration if turnover exceeds the prescribed threshold.

- **Partnership Enterprise**

A partnership involves two or more individuals who join together to conduct business and share profits and losses. The partnership can be formalized through a written agreement. The agreement is governed by the Indian Partnership Act, 1932 for general partnerships, and Limited Liability Partnership Act, 2008 for LLPs.

The Key features are

1. Minimum of 2 and maximum of 20 partners (for a general partnership). The maximum number of members that can exist in partnership is 10 in case of a firm carrying on banking business and 100 in case of any other business.
2. Profits and liabilities are shared based on the clause enumerated in partnership agreement/deed.
3. The partners are jointly and severally liable for the debts of the business (except in the case of LLP).
4. There are three types of partnerships (1) General Partnership: All partners share liability and control. (2) Limited Partnership LP: Includes both general partners (with unlimited liability) and limited partners (with liability only up to their capital contribution). (3) Limited Liability Partnership (LLP): A hybrid model combining elements of partnerships and corporations, where partners have limited liability like shareholders in a company. LLPs are governed by the Limited Liability Partnership Act, 2008. The partners' liability is restricted to the amount of their contribution to the LLP.

Advantages-

1. Pooling of resources and expertise from multiple partners.
2. Shared responsibility, allowing for more specialization.
3. Easy to form and manage.
4. Flexibility in operations and internal structure.

Disadvantages-

1. Unlimited liability for general partners.
2. Disagreements among partners can lead to business instability.
3. Difficulty in raising capital compared to corporations.
4. The partnership may dissolve if one partner leaves or dies.

The partnership agreement/deed can be executed in a place, within the partners in a non-judicial stamp paper of different value as prescribed by different states in compliance to Indian stamp act 1899. It is however desirable to get the partnership deed registered with registrar of firms or such other authorities prescribed, to enable the partnership deed enforceable in court of law in case of any dispute within the partners.

While opening current account of the enterprise in Banks, the registered partnership deed is more preferred as compared to non-registered partnership deed.

This form of constitution does not have any better legal status than the proprietary concern. It also gets dissolved in the event of retirement, death, insolvent, insane, being lunatic, being insane of any partners. This means that the existing account of such constitution maintained with Banks must be closed and new account must be opened. Books of accounts and all the credit limits must be novo examined and sanctioned after conducting due diligence of the new partners who joined and/or the ability of the reconstituted firm to discharge the liabilities of the firm.

There are no restrictions on the borrowing powers of a partnership firm, provided that no other partnership firm is partner in another firm.

As per the provisions of sec 32 of Indian Partnership act 1932, a minor can be considered as partnership with the consent of all the partners, but the minor will not be liable for losses of the firm. Within six months after the minor attains the age of majority, the minor will have the option to repudiate his liability as a partner otherwise minor will be held liable as a partner of the firm from the date he was admitted for the benefits of partnership.

- **Limited Liability Partnership (LLP)**

LLP is considered as an alternative business constitution that provides the benefit of the limited liability but allows its members the flexibility of organizing their constitutional structure as partnership based on mutual agreement. Government of India enacted the Limited Liability Partnership act 2008(LLP Act) on January 07, 2009 and notified the various provisions of the act on 31st March 2009. Government of India also notified the Limited Liability Partnership rules 2009 (LLP rules) in context to registration and operational procedures.

The Key features are

1. LLP is an entity separate from its partners. It will have perpetual succession. Indian Partnership Act 1932 shall not be applicable to LLPs.
2. LLP has to form with a minimum of two persons. The act does not restrict the benefit of LLP structure to certain classes of professionals only and would be available for use of any enterprises which fulfils the prerequisites of the act.
3. LLP gives the benefit of limited liability like joint stock companies, but would allow its members the liberty of managing their internal structure as a partnership based on the LLP agreement.
4. A registered LLP has the power of suing and being sued; and also acquiring, owing, and developing or disposing off property.
5. There are provisions for inter conversion of LLP into Pvt limited company.

Advantages-

1. Limited liability for all partners.
2. Flexible structure and operational freedom.
3. Less stringent regulatory requirements compared to a private company.
4. Ease of management with less formalities.
5. Can convert into a private limited company later if needed.

<u>Disadvantages-</u>
1. Limited ability to raise large amounts of capital (as in private limited companies).
2. Partners cannot transfer ownership as freely as in a private company.
3. Requires formal registration and filing of annual returns.

In order that small enterprises have a new form of business organization combining the advantages of a partnership, without the hassles of a private limited liability company, a Limited liability partnership was contemplated. While LLP will be a separate legal entity, liable to the full extent of its assets and liabilities of the partners would be limited to their agreed contribution in the LLP. Further no partner would be liable on account of the independent or unauthorized actions of other partners. Thus, allowing individual partners to be shielded from joint liability created by another partner's wrongful business decisions or misconduct.

- **Joint Stock Companies**

Joint Stock Companies which comprise of Private limited companies and public limited companies have a legal entity separate from its owners (Shareholders). Joint Stock companies gain the legal status by being registered under companies act 1956 (amended 2013) with registrar of companies located in each state headquarters.

Ownership and Management is an extraordinary feature of a joint stock company. Company's shareholders are the owners of the company but on the event if it is not possible to exercise day-to-day rights of the shareholders of the company, in that case shareholders appoint their representatives as Directors who is part of Board of Management. Transferability of shares is another feature of a joint stock company. The transfer of shares is governed by the guidelines of Security and Exchange board of India.

Being an artificial legal person, a joint stock company can have a perpetual legal existence and cannot be closed by mere wish of shareholders. The existence of a joint stock company can be extinguished after complying with all legal formalities.

A joint stock company can be "Public" or "Private". The distinctions are as follows:

<u>Public Limited Company (Ltd.)</u>
A public limited company is similar to a private limited company, but it can offer its shares to the public through stock exchanges. It is typically used by larger businesses that need to raise capital by issuing shares to the public.
1. Minimum of 7 members and no maximum limit on shareholders.
2. "Public limited company is defined in sec 3(1)(iv) of the act and it means a company which is not a private limited company.

1. Minimum paid up capital is 5 lac or such higher capital as may be prescribed
2. Limited liability for shareholders.
3. Shares can be listed on a stock exchange.
4. Requires a large amount of regulatory compliance.
5. Memorandum and article of association are prepared and the purpose and objectives of such association and for which the company is formed should be spelt out.
6. The registrar of company issues the certificate of incorporation and certificate of commencement of business to public limited company. Please note that certificate of commencement of business is not required in case it is private limited company.

Private Limited Company

A private limited company is a separate legal entity with limited liability for its shareholders. It is owned by a small group of individuals and cannot publicly trade its shares.

1. Minimum of 2 and a maximum of 200 members (shareholders).
2. Limited liability for shareholders (liability is limited to the amount invested in shares).
3. Requires at least two directors, and one of them must be a resident of India.
4. The company is a distinct legal entity from its owners.
5. Cannot raise funds from the public or list its shares on a stock exchange.
6. The minimum paid up capital is one lac

Private limited company is preferred by those who wish to take the advantage of limited liability, but at the same time desire to keep control over the business within a limited circle and maintain the privacy of business.

- **One Person Company (OPC)**

Section 2(62) of Companies Act defines a one-person company as a company that has only one person as to its member. Furthermore, members of a company are nothing but subscribers to its memorandum of association, or its shareholders. So, an OPC is effectively a company that has only one shareholder as its member. Such companies are generally created when there is only one founder/promoter for the business. Entrepreneurs whose businesses lie in early stages prefer to create OPCs instead of sole proprietorship business because of the several advantages that OPCs offer.

A sole proprietorship form of business might seem very similar to one-person companies because they both involve a single person owning the business, but they're actually exist some differences between them.

The main difference between the two is the nature of the liabilities they carry. Since an OPC is a separate legal entity distinguished from its promoter, it has its own assets and liabilities. The promoter is not personally liable to repay the debts of the company.

On the other hand, sole proprietorships and their proprietors are the same persons. So, the law allows attachment and sale of promoter's own assets in case of non-fulfilment of the business' liabilities.

The Key features are

1. Minimum of 1 member (sole proprietor) and 1 director.
2. Limited liability protection.
3. The nominee is required in case the sole member dies or becomes incapacitated.
4. Registered as a company, but operates with the flexibility of a sole proprietorship.

Advantages-

1. Limited liability protects the owner's personal assets.
2. No need to share control with others.
3. Suitable for small businesses and solo entrepreneurs who want the benefits of a corporate structure.
4. Easier to convert to a private limited company once the business grows.

Disadvantages-

1. Cannot have more than one member.
2. Not suitable for businesses requiring significant capital investment or large teams.
3. Stricter regulatory and compliance requirements than sole proprietorships.

- **Co-operative Societies**

A co-operative society is a voluntary association of individuals having common needs who join hands for the achievement of common economic interest. Its aim is to serve the interest of the poorer sections of society through the principle of self-help and mutual help. The main objective is to provide support to the members. Nobody joins a cooperative society to earn profit. People come forward as a group, pool their individual resources, utilize them in the best possible manner, and derive some common benefit out of it.

A Co-operative Society can be formed as per the provisions of the Co-operative Societies Act, 1912. At least ten persons above of 18 years, having the capacity to enter into a contract with common economic objectives, like farming, weaving, consuming, etc. can form a Co-operative Society.

The Key features are

1. Operated on the principle of "one member, one vote," regardless of the number of shares held.
2. Profits are shared equally or based on usage by the members.
3. A democratic and member-driven organization.

<u>Advantages-</u>
1. Members have equal voting rights.
2. Focus on mutual benefits and service, rather than profit maximization.
3. Tax exemptions on income derived from specific activities.

<u>Disadvantages-</u>
1. Limited access to external funding.
2. Management inefficiency can occur if the cooperative's membership is large.
3. May face challenges in maintaining a balance between democratic management and professional business practices.

- **Joint Hindu Family Business**

A joint Hindu family business (HUF) is a business organization in India where multiple generations of a Hindu family work together and own the business. The business is owned and run by the members of a Hindu Undivided Family (HUF). The family members are called co-parceners. The eldest member of the family, called the Karta, is the head of the business and is responsible for its management and finances. The Karta makes decisions that bind the other members. The liability of each member is limited to their share of the business's co-parcenery property, except for the Karta.

The family carrying an ancestral business consisting of all the above is a legal entity. The Karta shall execute and determine on behalf of the family. If the Karta is disabled or absent from the station for a long time, any major co-parcener can enter into transaction as permitted by JHF. The business continues even after the Karta's death, as the next eldest member becomes the new Karta. Membership is limited to people born into the family or by marriage to a male member of the family.

<u>The Key features are</u>
1. The business is owned and managed by a joint family.
2. The Karta has complete control over the management of the business.
3. Profits are shared among family members.

<u>Advantages</u>
1. Family members share the responsibility.
2. No need for formal agreements or regulatory filings.
3. The family can continue the business across generations.

<u>Disadvantage</u>
1. Only applicable to families following Hindu law.
2. Limited to family-based businesses, and management can be complex as the family grows.
3. The Karta has unlimited liability.

- **Franchise**
  1. A franchise model allows a business (franchisor) to grant another party (franchisee) the rights to operate using the franchisor's brand, trademark, and business methods. The legal framework of business model is based on a franchise agreement between the franchisor and franchisee.
  2. The franchisee operates a business under the franchisor's brand. The franchisee pays an initial fee and ongoing royalty payments to the franchisor.

- **Non-Profit Organizations (NPO)**
  1. An NPO, or non-profit organization, is a legal entity that's primarily focused on promoting the public good, rather than making a profit. NPOs are established for charitable, educational, religious, or social purposes, and the income generated is reinvested to fulfill the mission of the organization.
  2. The constitution of such organization is governed by the Societies Registration Act, 1860, Indian Trusts Act, 1882, and Section 8 of the Companies Act, 2013.
  3. NPOs are dedicated to a specific cause or social issue. They use their income to create and maintain programs that benefit their cause or community.

CHAPTER-4
UNIT SET-UP & PROJECT REPORT

Most business activities can be classified in the following broad categories. It is therefore important and essential for an entrepreneur to understand under which category his/her business activity falls.

Industries can be classified into multiple categories depending on the classification system used. However, the most common and widely recognized systems group industries into four main categories or sectors. These broad categories are as follows:

1. **Primary Sector (Extraction and Resource-based Industries)**: This sector involves industries that extract natural resources from the Earth or sea, Examples: Agriculture, mining, forestry, fishing, and oil extraction. These are focused on the extraction or harvesting of raw materials directly from nature.

2. **Secondary Sector (Manufacturing and Processing Industries)**: This sector involves industries that take raw materials and transform them into finished goods or products. Examples: Manufacturing, construction, food processing, chemical production, and the production of consumer goods like electronics and automobiles. The characteristic of this type of industries Involves industrial activity, production, and assembly of goods, typically requiring labor, machinery, and factories.

3. **Tertiary Sector (Service Industries)**: This sector involves industries that provide services rather than goods. The tertiary sector supports the primary and secondary sectors, and is often the largest sector in developed economies. Examples: Retail, hospitality, healthcare, education, financial services, insurance, real estate, IT services, transportation, and entertainment. This type of industry provides intangible products (services) that support the functioning of society and businesses.

4. **Quaternary Sector (Knowledge and Information-based Industries):** This sector focuses on knowledge-based activities, including research and development (R&D), technology, consulting, and information services. Examples: Information technology, education, financial planning, biotechnology, scientific research, consulting, and media. Such industries include and involves the generation, dissemination, and use of information and intellectual property.

5. **Quinary Sector (High-level Decision-making and Creative Services):** This sector includes high-level decision-making and services that focus on creativity, innovation, and knowledge generation. Examples: Scientific research, high-level management (executives, policymakers), non-profit activities, education, healthcare (e.g., advanced medical services), and media. Such industry involves highly skilled and creative work, often related to problem-solving, decision-making, and intellectual capital.

After having finalized the product and its category, an entrepreneur must prepare a comprehensive project report and modify/upgrade it from time to time.

A project report is a structured document that provides an overview of a specific project, its objectives, methods, progress, results, and conclusions. It serves to communicate key information to stakeholders such as project sponsors, managers, team members, and external parties. The report typically outlines the purpose of the project, the approach taken, the outcomes achieved, and any recommendations or lessons learned. A well-prepared project report also provides a reference for future work and decision-making.

Key Components of a Project Report

Title Page - The title page includes the project title, the name of the project team or individual, the date of incorporation, and any other relevant identifying information. It sets the tone for the report and provides initial context.

Executive Summary - The executive summary offers a brief synopsis of the entire report, summarizing the key points such as the project's objectives, methodology, outcomes, and conclusions. It is usually concise (about 150–200 words) and allows the reader to quickly understand the purpose and results of the project.

Introduction - The introduction section explains the context of the project. It includes A brief description of the problem, need, or opportunity that the project addresses. Clear and concise statements about what the project aimed to achieve. Defines the boundaries of the project, what it will cover, and any limitations. Explains why the project matters and how it contributes to the overall goals of the organization or stakeholders.

Methodology - This section outlines the approach used to carry out the project. It includes whether the project involved data collection, experiments, surveys, or case studies. Describes any software, tools, or technologies used. Includes timelines, milestones, and how the project was managed and lists the human, financial, and physical resources required for the project.

Results and Analysis - In this section, the results of the project are presented in detail. This may involve Charts, graphs, tables, or descriptive text that present the outcomes of the project. Interpretation of the results and what they mean in the context of the project's objectives and any obstacles encountered during the project and how they were addressed.

Discussion - The discussion section provides a deeper analysis of the results and their implications. This includes How the actual results compare with initial predictions or goals. What the results reveal about the problem or opportunity the project addressed. Insights gained from the process that could be applied to future projects and suggestions for next steps or actions based on the findings.

Conclusion - The conclusion summarizes the entire project and its outcomes. It highlights the key achievements and reinforces the significance of the project. It also provides a final assessment of the project's success in meeting its objectives.

<u>References</u> - A list of all sources, research papers, books, websites, and any other materials referenced during the project.

<u>Appendices</u> - Appendices include any supplementary information such as raw data, additional charts, or detailed explanations that support the main text of the report.

A project report is essential for several reasons. It provides a record of the project's journey, which can be referred to for future analysis or audits. It communicates the project's goals, activities, results, and challenges to stakeholders, ensuring transparency and accountability. By analyzing results, a project report helps assess whether the project met its objectives and delivered value.

The insights from a project report guide management or stakeholders in making informed decisions about future actions, projects, or improvements.

A project report is a critical tool for summarizing and reflecting on the progress, challenges, and outcomes of a project. It acts as both a formal record and a means of communication to stakeholders, helping to ensure the success of current and future projects.

By documenting the approach, results, and lessons learned, a project report serves as a valuable resource for continuous improvement and informed decision-making.

CHAPTER-5
STATUTORY REGISTRATIONS

Government of India has put in revised classification of MSME with effect from 1st July 2020. As far as investment in plant & machinery and equipment and annual turnover is concerned it is being revised as under:

Classification	Micro Enterprises	Small Enterprises	Medium Enterprises
Manufacturing Enterprises and Enterprises rendering Services	Investment in Plant and Machinery or Equipment: Not more than Rs.1 crore and Annual Turnover; not more than Rs. 5 crores	Investment in Plant and Machinery or Equipment: Not more than Rs.10 crore and Annual Turnover; not more than Rs. 50 crores	Investment in Plant and Machinery or Equipment: Not more than Rs.50 crore and Annual Turnover; not more than Rs. 250 crores

MSMEs in India must ensure compliance with various statutory registrations to operate legally, ensure employee welfare, protect intellectual property, and qualify for government incentives. The registration process has been simplified in recent years, with many procedures now being digitized, making it easier for businesses to meet regulatory requirements. Statutory registrations for MSMEs in India ensure that businesses comply with local and national regulations, safeguard employee welfare, and qualify for government schemes and incentives. These registrations, ranging from MSME registration to labor law compliance, are essential for MSMEs to operate legally and efficiently. With the growing importance of MSMEs in the Indian economy, these registrations also help businesses build credibility, access credit, and tap into growth opportunities.

In India, Micro, Small, and Medium Enterprises (MSMEs) play a crucial role in the economy, contributing significantly to employment, innovation, and exports. To operate legally and access benefits such as subsidies, financial support, and preferential treatment under government schemes, MSMEs are required to complete several statutory registrations and compliance procedures. Here's a detailed overview of the key statutory registrations for MSMEs in India.

- **MSME Registration (Udyam Registration)**
  1. The purpose of MSME registration under the Udyam Registration scheme is essential for businesses to avail various benefits like subsidies, easy access to credit, protection against delayed payments, and eligibility for government schemes.
  2. All businesses involved in manufacturing, processing, or service activities can apply for Udyam Registration. It is done online via the Udyam portal. The process requires the Aadhar number (for individual proprietors), PAN card, GSTIN (if applicable), business details, and bank account information. To access for Udyam registration link one can, visit *http://udyamregistration.gov.in*

- **Goods and Services Tax (GST) Registration**
  1. Businesses with an annual turnover exceeding ₹40 lakh for goods or ₹20 lakh for services need to register for GST. GST registration is mandatory for businesses involved in the supply of goods or services, enabling them to collect and remit tax.
  2. MSMEs must apply online via the GST portal. The application requires PAN, Aadhar, business details, and bank information. To access for GST registration link one can, visit *https://services.gst.gov.in*

- **Trade License**
  1. A trade license is issued by the local municipal authority to regulate business operations, ensuring compliance with local laws related to health, safety, and zoning. All businesses that engage in commercial activities (like shops, manufacturing units, or service centers) must obtain a trade license.
  2. Registration with the local municipal authority is required, and the application process may vary depending on the state or municipality.

- **Shop and Establishment Act Registration**
  1. This registration governs the working conditions, rights, and welfare of employees in commercial establishments. It ensures compliance with labor laws concerning working hours, wages, and leave provisions. It is mandatory for any business (e.g., shops, restaurants, service providers) to register under the Shop and Establishment Act.
  2. The application must be filed with the state's labor department, which issues a certificate after inspection.

- **Employees' Provident Fund (EPF) Registration**
  1. MSMEs with 20 or more employees are required to register under the Employees' Provident Fund Organization (EPFO). The EPF scheme provides retirement benefits to employees, with both the employer and employee contributing a percentage of the salary.
  2. The registration can be done through the EPFO portal, and businesses must regularly deposit employee and employer contributions. To access for EPFO registration link one can, visit *https://unifiedportal-emp.epfindia.gov.in*

- **Import Export Code (IEC) Registration**
  1. Any MSME involved in import or export must obtain an IEC. The IEC is a unique code issued by the Directorate General of Foreign Trade (DGFT) that enables businesses to engage in international trade.
  2. The IEC can be applied online through the DGFT portal with necessary documents such as PAN, bank details, and business registration documents.
  3. To access for IEC registration link one can, visit https://dgft.gov.in/(Proceed with registration process by clicking on Login > Register > Register as "Importer/Exporter". After registration, Go to My Dashboard → Importer Exporter Code (IEC) → Apply for IEC)

- **Factory License**
  1. All manufacturing units need to obtain this license. The factory license ensures that a manufacturing unit complies with safety, health, and labor laws stipulated under the Factories Act, 1948.
  2. It can be applied to the local factory inspectorate or labor department, depending on the business location.

- **Food Safety and Standards Authority of India (FSSAI) License**
  1. MSMEs involved in food processing, packaging, or distribution must register under the FSSAI. The FSSAI license ensures that food businesses meet safety and hygiene standards set by the Food Safety and Standards Act, 2006.
  2. Registration is done online on the FSSAI portal, with different categories of registration based on the scale of operations.

- **Pollution Control License**
  1. Manufacturing MSMEs generating emissions or waste need to obtain a license from the State Pollution Control Board. For businesses involved in industrial production, this license ensures compliance with environmental laws related to air, water, and noise pollution.
  2. The application is submitted to the local pollution control board.

- **Patent and Trademark Registration**
  1. MSMEs seeking to protect their innovations or trademarks should register for patents and trademarks. Protects the intellectual property of MSMEs, including inventions, product designs, and brand names.
  2. Registration is done through the Intellectual Property India office.

- **Labor Law Compliance**
  1. MSMEs with employees must comply with these labor laws and maintain proper records. Compliance with various labor laws like the Minimum Wages Act, Payment of Bonus Act, and the Industrial Disputes Act is required for MSMEs to ensure employee welfare and avoid disputes. Regular compliance with the Department of Labor and filing reports is necessary.

CHAPTER-6
GOVERNMENT SUPPORT & POLICY

Several changes have occurred in the global economy since the 1990s. Economies have become more interdependent, and markets have become more open and competitive. A more rule based multilateral trade regime, within the framework of World trade organization (WTO) agreements, is in place.

India's economic policies are in the process of being restructured, through the second-generation reforms, to adjust to this emerging challenges. The main emphasis of future policy will be to continue to promote the growth of MSME sector through focused interventions.

MSME in India constitute an important segment of Indian economy. The contribution of MSME alone has been greater than 8% to GDP and 45% to Industrial production. It is also the second largest provider of employment after Agriculture. MSMEs also contribute to 40% of total exports directly and a significant number of exports indirectly through large trading houses or third parties. The sector is expected to grow 20% YoY with 90% of the industrial units.

The Government of India has enacted the Micro Small and Medium Enterprises development act on June 16, 2006. The act is popularly known as MSMED act 2006. Both manufacturing and service sectors have been included in the definition of MSME, apart from extending the scope to medium enterprises. On 9 May 2007, subsequent to an amendment of the Government of India (Allocation of Business) Rules, 1961, erstwhile Ministry of Small-Scale Industries and the Ministry of Agro and Rural Industries were merged to form the Ministry of Micro, Small and Medium Enterprises (M/o MSME). This Ministry now designs policies and promotes/ facilitates programs, projects and schemes and monitors their implementation with a view to assisting MSMEs and helping them to scale up.

In accordance with the provisions of MSMED act 2006 the Micro small and medium enterprises have been classified in two categories:

1. Manufacturing enterprises – The enterprises engaged in the manufacture or production of goods related to any industry specified in first schedule to the industries development and regulation act 1951. The manufacturing enterprises are symbolized in terms of investment in Plant & machinery.
2. Service Enterprises – The enterprises engaged in providing or rendering of services and symbolized in terms of investment in equipment.

The objective of the MSMED act 2006, as spelt out in the preamble of the act, are to provide for facilitating the promotion and development and enhancing the competitiveness of Micro Small and medium Enterprises and for matters connected or incidental thereto. The MSMED act 2006 contains six chapters. Ministry of Micro, Small & Medium Enterprises (M/o MSME) envision a vibrant MSME sector by promoting growth and development of the MSME Sector, including Khadi, Village and Coir Industries, in cooperation with concerned Ministries/Departments, State Governments and other Stakeholders, through providing support to existing enterprises and encouraging creation of new enterprises.

Khadi is the proud legacy of our national freedom movement and the father of the nation. Khadi and Village Industries (KVI) are two national heritages of India. One of the most significant aspects of KVI in Indian economy is that it creates employment at a very low per capita investment. The KVI Sector not only serves the basic needs of processed goods of the vast rural sector of the country, but also provides sustainable employment to rural artisans. KVI today represents an exquisite, heritage product, which is 'ethnic' as well as ethical. It has a potentially strong clientele among the middle and upper echelons of society.

Coir Industry is an agro-based traditional industry, which originated in the state of Kerala and proliferated to the other coconut producing states like Tamil Nadu, Karnataka, Andhra Pradesh, Orissa, West Bengal, Maharashtra, Assam, Tripura, etc. It is an export-oriented industry and has greater potential to enhance exports by value addition through technological interventions and diversified products like Coir Geotextiles etc. The acceptability of Coir products has increased rapidly due to its 'environmentally friendly' image.

The vision and mission of Ministry of Micro, Small and Medium Enterprises is for sustainable development of globally competitive MSME sector as an engine of growth for the Indian economy. The ministry also works for the promotion and development of Khadi, Village and coir industries so as to create new enterprises and more employment opportunities. The long term goal of the ministry is to enhance manufacturing base in the country by improving performance of MSMEs through skill and entrepreneurship development.

The main functions of the ministry are: -

1. Facilitation and credit flow to MSMEs
2. Improving competitiveness of MSMEs
3. Improve manufacturing base through upgradation of technology
4. Promotion of MSMEs through cluster bases approach
5. Marketing support to MSMEs
6. Skill development and entrepreneurship development training.
7. Creation of new Micro Enterprises through Prime Minister's Employment Generation Program (PMEGP)
8. Growth and development of Khadi and Village Industries (KVI) sector
9. Growth and development of Coir Industry

There are few other organizations which are attached to Ministry of Micro Small and medium enterprises in order to ensure smooth implementation of Government support. These organizations are as under: -

Office of Development Commissioner (MSME)
Development Commissionerate implements the policies and various programs/schemes for providing infrastructure and support services to MSMEs. The Office of the Development Commissioner [O/o DC (MSME)] is an attached office of the Ministry, headed by the Additional Secretary & Development Commissioner (AS & DC), MSME. It functions through a network of MSME-Development Institutes (DI), Regional Testing Centers, Footwear Training Institutes, Production Centers, Field Testing Stations and specialized institutes. It renders services such as:

1. Advising the Government in Policy formulation for the promotion and development of MSMEs.
2. Providing techno-economic and managerial consultancy, common facilities and extension services to MSME units.
3. Providing facilities for technology upgradation, modernization, quality improvement and infrastructure.
4. Developing Human Resources through training and skill upgradation.
5. Providing economic information services.

Khadi Village Industries Commission (KVIC)
Khadi & Village Industries Commission (KVIC) established under the Khadi and Village Industries Commission Act, 1956 (61 of 1956), is a statutory organization under the aegis of the Ministry of MSME. The main objectives of KVIC includes providing employment in rural areas; economic objective of producing saleable articles; and wider objective of creating self-reliance amongst people and building up a strong rural community spirit. The functions of KVIC as prescribed under the KVIC Act, 1956 (61 of 1956) and Rules made there under, include:

1. To plan and organize training of persons employed or desirous of seeking employment in khadi and village industries.
2. To build up directly or through specified agencies reserves of raw materials and implements and supply them or arrange supply of raw materials and implements to persons engaged or likely to be engaged in production of hand spun yarn or khadi or village industries at such rates as the Commission may decide.
3. To encourage and assist in the creation of common service facilities for the processing of raw materials or semi-finished goods and otherwise facilitate production and marketing of khadi or products of village industries.
4. To promote the sale and marketing of khadi or products of village industries or handicrafts and for this purpose forge links with established marketing agencies wherever necessary and feasible.
5. To encourage and promote research in the technology used in khadi and village industries, including the use of non-conventional energy and electric power with a view to increasing productivity, eliminating drudgery and otherwise enhancing their competitive capacity and to arrange for dissemination of salient results obtained from such research.
6. To undertake directly or through other agencies, studies of the problems of khadi or village industries.
7. To provide financial assistance directly or through specified agencies to institutions or persons engaged in the development and operation of khadi or village industries and guide them through supply of designs, prototypes and other technical information, for the purpose of producing goods and services for which there is effective demand in the opinion of the Commission.
8. To undertake directly or through specified agencies, experiments or pilot projects which in the opinion of the Commission, are necessary for the development of khadi and village industries.
9. To establish and maintain separate organizations for the purpose of carrying out any or all of the above matters.

Coir Board

India is the largest coir producer in the world accounting for more than 80 per cent of the total world production of coir fibre. The coir sector in India is very diverse and involves households, co-operatives, NGOs, manufacturers and exporters. This is the best example of producing beautiful artifacts, handicrafts and utility products from coconut husks which is otherwise a waste. The coir industry employs more than 7.00 lakh persons of whom a majority are from rural areas belonging to the economically weaker sections of society. Nearly 80% of the coir workers in the fibre extraction and spinning sectors are women. The Coir Board is tasked with promoting the overall development of the coir industry and improvement of the living conditions of the workers engaged in this traditional industry.

The Coir Board is a statutory body established under the Coir Industry Act, 1953 for promoting the overall development of the coir industry and improvement of the living conditions of the workers engaged in this traditional industry. The functions of the Coir Board for the development of coir industry, inter-alia, include:

1. Promoting exports of coir yarn and coir products and carrying on propaganda for that purpose.
2. Regulating under the supervision of the Central Government the production of husks, coir yarn and coir products by registering coir spindles and looms for manufacturing coir products as also manufacturers of coir products.
3. Undertaking, assisting or encouraging scientific, technological and economic research and maintaining and assisting in the maintenance of one or more research institutes.
4. Collecting statistics from manufacturers of and dealers in coir products and from other persons as may be prescribed, on any matter relating to the coir industry and the publication of statistics so collected.
5. Fixing grade standards are arranged when necessary for inspection of fibre, coir yarn and coir products.
6. Improving the marketing of coconut husk, coir fibre, coir yarn and coir products in India and elsewhere and preventing unfair competitions.
7. Setting up or assisting in the setup of factories for the producers of coir products with the aid of power.
8. Promoting co-operative organization among producers of husks, coir fibre and coir yarn and manufactures of coir products.
9. Ensuring remunerative return to producers of husks coir fibre and coir yarn and manufacturers of coir products.
10. Advising on all matters relating to the development of the coir industry.

National Small Industries Corporation Limited (NSIC)

The mission of NSIC is "To promote and support Micro, Small and Medium Enterprises by providing integrated support services encompassing, Marketing, Finance, Technology and other Services." The vision of NSIC is "To be premier organization fostering the growth of Micro, Small and Medium Enterprises in the country."

NSIC provides technical support to MSMEs through 'NSIC Technical Services Centres' (NTSCs) and a number of TICs & LBIs spread across the country. The range of technical services provided through these centres includes skill development in Hi-Tech as well as conventional trades, material and product testing.

One of the programs being implemented by NSIC is to create self-employment opportunities by imparting training in entrepreneurship building to the unemployed people who want to set up new small business enterprises in any of the manufacturing/ services sectors or seek employment opportunities. For this purpose, NSIC has started a new initiative by entering into franchisee arrangements with private partners interested in setting up of Training-cum-Incubation centers (NSIC-TIC) at various locations across the country under Public-Private Partnership (PPP) mode.

The National Small Industries Corporation Ltd. (NSIC) is an ISO 9001-2015 certified Government of India Enterprise under Ministry of Micro, Small and Medium Enterprises (MSME). NSIC has been working to promote aid and foster the growth of micro, small and medium enterprises in the country. NSIC performs three distinct categories of activities in order to fulfill its mission. It runs a number of schemes, and is also an implementing partner for a number of schemes of the Ministry of MSME. These schemes/ activities include:
1. Consortia and Tender Marketing
2. Credit Support
3. Raw Material Distribution
4. Single Point Registration Scheme (SPRS)
5. NSIC Technical Services Centers
6. E-Marketing/ Digital Services facilitation for MSMEs
7. National Scheduled Caste and Scheduled Tribe Hub.

National Institute for micro, Small and Medium Enterprises (NIMSME)
The primary objective of NIMSME was to be the trainer of trainers. Today, with the technological development and ever-changing market scenario, the organization's involvement has undergone changes too. From being merely trainers, NIMSME has widened its scope of activities to consultancy, research, extension and information services.

The existing Jamnalal Bajaj Central Research Institute (JBCRI), Wardha was revamped with the help of IIT, Delhi as a national level institute under the Ministry of MSME in October 2008 called Mahatma Gandhi Institute for Rural Industrialization (MGIRI).

In line with the national objective of economic development through industrialization, and based on the expertise that is available, the Institute has identified thrust areas that need emphasis and exploration. These are: Entrepreneurship Development, Technology Up-gradation & Transfer, Policy Issues, NGO Networking, Environment Concerns, Cluster Development, Management Consultancy, Quality Management Services, Financial Services, and Information Services. Enterprise promotion and entrepreneurship development being the central focus of NIMSME's functions, the Institute's competencies converge on the following aspects: -

1. Enabling enterprise creation.
2. Capacity building for enterprise growth and sustainability.
3. Creation, development and dissemination of enterprise knowledge.
4. Diagnostic and development studies for policy formulation.
5. Empowering the under-privileged through enterprise creation.
6. Turning new corners in Information Technology.
7. Spotlighting of topical issues through conferences, seminars, etc.
8. Greater attention to need-based programs.
9. Shift towards client driven approach and innovative interventions.
10. Program evaluation.
11. Emphasis on research publications.

The Reserve Bank of India has played a significant role in building up the requisite institutional structure to meet the needs of credit requirements of MSMEs. The guidelines issued by RBI to various Banks and financial institutions cover aspects relating to timely and adequate sanction of working capital financial requirement, rejection of proposals, co-ordination between commercial banks and state financial corporations, submission of periodical reports to boards of Banks/Fis with respect to credit assistance to MSMEs.
Some all-India lending Institutions are as under:

Small Industries Development Bank of India: Small Industries Development Bank of India (SIDBI) set up on 2nd April 1990 under an Act of Indian Parliament, acts as the Principal Financial Institution for Promotion, Financing and Development of the Micro, Small and Medium Enterprise (MSME) sector as well as for co-ordination of functions of institutions engaged in similar activities. The institution has emerged as a single window for meeting the financial and developmental needs of the MSME sector to make it strong, vibrant and globally competitive.

SIDBI plays a proactive role in promotion and development of MSMEs to address various non- financial challenges faced by them. SIDBI aims at innovating for wider impact and to benefit MSEs in both "setting up" and "stepping up", thereby leading to economic growth of the country.

"Mission Swavalamban" is an umbrella program of SIDBI for aspiring, livelihood, micro and small entrepreneurs. Under the mission, SIDBI spreads entrepreneurship culture and turn youth from "Job seekers" to "Job creators"; restrict rural migration to urban area and promote sustainable livelihood opportunities with thrust on bottom of pyramid, unserved/underserved pockets/ segments and overall MSMEs through various novel initiatives.

Although SIDBI has started functioning as a refinancing institution but now it provides assistance to MSME units directly. The important supports provided by SIDBI are as under:

1. Term loans are provided for setting up new projects and its modernization, diversification, expansion etc. It also provides working capital term loans, bill discounting facilities, equity, debt and hybrid finance.
2. SIDBI provides resource support to Institutions/ Non-Banking finance companies to facilitate channelizing assistance to a large number of MSMEs and infrastructure projects having linkages to MSMEs.
3. SIDBI extends nodal agency services to the Government of India for schemes sponsored by its various ministries for encouraging implementation of modernization and technology upgradation by manufacturing units in the MSME sector such as CREDIT LINKED CAPITAL SUBSIDY SCHEME (CLCSS), TECHNOLOGY UPGRADATION FUND SCHEME (TUFS) for textile Industry and INTEGRATED DEVELOPMENT OF LEATHER SECTO SCHEME (IDLSS).
4. To meet the micro credit demand, SIDBI constituted a specialized department called SIDBI foundation for micro credit, to create a national network of strong viable and sustainable Micro finance Institution from the formal and informal sectors to provide microfinance services to the poor, especially women.
5. The indirect assistance of SIDBI consists of refinance and resource support in the form of short-term loans/line of credit to primary lending institutions, comprising state level financial Institutions and Banks.
6. SIDBI has also created a subsidiary named SIDBI VENTURE CAPITAL LIMITED (SVCL) in order to support innovative, knowledge-based first-generation entrepreneurs having neither equity nor collateral.

Export Import Bank of India (EXIM) – The EXIM Bank of India set up by an act of Parliament for the purpose of financing, facilitating and promoting India's foreign trade. It also extends support to MSMEs in a big way. EXIM Bank has various facilities under its schemes for pre-shipment, post-shipment, investment abroad, advisory services, import finance, export product development, export promotion and export marketing.

Ministry of Micro small & medium enterprises has implemented number of schemes, aimed at financial assistance, technology assistance and upgradation, infrastructure development, skill development and training and enhancing competitiveness and market assistance of MSME.

The key feature of the schemes are as below:

PRIME MINISTER'S EMPLOYMENT GENERATION PROGRAMME (PMEGP)

<u>OBJECTIVE</u>

1. The scheme aims to provide financial assistance to set-up self-employment ventures and generate sustainable employment opportunities in rural as well as in urban areas.
2. The scheme also gives emphasis for sustainable and continuous employment opportunities for rural and unemployed youth as well as prospective traditional artisans and thereby halt occupational migrations.

<u>KEY BENEFITS</u>

1. Credit linked subsidy program for setting up new micro enterprise in non-farm sector.
2. Margin money subsidy ranges from 15% to 35% of project cost for projects up to Rs 50 lakh in manufacturing sector and Rs 20 lakh in service sector.
3. For beneficiaries belonging to special categories such as SC/ST/Women/Minorities/Ex-servicemen/Transgenders/Aspirational districts/NER, the margin money subsidy is 35% in rural areas and 25% in urban areas.

<u>SCHEME APPLICABLE FOR</u>

1. Any individual above 18 years of age can apply.

<u>DETAILED INFORMATION</u>

1. The own contribution of the beneficiary is 10% of the project cost in case of General category, and 5% of project cost in case of special category such as SC/ST/Women/Minorities/Ex-servicemen/Transgenders/Aspirational districts/NER beneficiaries.
2. If the application for loan is approved, the bank sanction and release the balance amount of 90 to 95 percent of the total project cost suitably for setting up of the units by the beneficiaries.
3. In order to have sustainability of the projects/units set up under the scheme, support services are also provided in the form of backward and forward linkages by organizing events like workshops, EDP training to the beneficiaries, exhibitions etc.
4. Government of India has introduced online process for flow of applications and disbursement of margin money directly to financing branches.
5. Online application form is mandatory for individuals on the e-portal. The application form/PMEGP MIS portal is mobile friendly. SMS/e-mail alerts are sent to the applicants automatically by the system or by the concerned official at each stage.
6. Model project report of different activities have been put up on PMEGP e-portal for the benefit of potential beneficiaries.
7. To increase the registration of MSMEs in the country, the government has undertaken measures for PMEGP units to adopt the Udyog Aadhar Memorandum/Udyam Registration.

<u>HOW TO APPLY</u>

1. Apply on *https://www.kviconline.gov.in/pmegpeportal/pmegphome*

SECOND LOAN FOR UPGRADATION OF THE EXISTING PMEGP/REGP/MUDRA UNITS

<u>OBJECTIVE</u>

1. With an objective to assist existing units for expansion and upgradation, the scheme provides financial assistance to successful/well performing units.
2. The scheme also caters to the needs of the entrepreneurs for bringing new technology/automation so as to modernize the existing unit.

<u>KEY BENEFITS</u>

1. Maximum subsidy would be 15% of the project cost (20% for NER and hill states). The balance amount of the total project cost is provided by banks as term loan.

<u>SCHEMES APPLICABLE FOR</u>

1. Existing well performing PMEGP/REGP/MUDRA units

<u>DETAILED INFORMATION</u>

1. Further financial assistance scheme for expansion/upgrade the existing PMEGP/REGP/MUDRA units for manufacturing and services/trading units from the year 2018-19
2. The maximum cost of the project under manufacturing sector for upgradation is Rs 100 crores and Rs 25 lakh under service/trading sector
3. Maximum subsidy would be 15% of the project cost (20% for NER and Hill states) i.e. Rs 15 lakh in Non-NER and Rs 20 lakh for NER hill states. The balance amount of the total project cost shall be provided by Banks as term loan.
4. All existing units financed under PMEGP/MUDRA scheme whose margin money claim has been adjusted and the first loan availed has been repaid in stipulated time are eligible to avail the benefits.
5. The unit should have been making profit for the last 3 years.
6. Beneficiary can apply to the same financing bank, which sanctioned the loan for their unit, or to any other financing bank, which is willing to extend credit facility for second loan.
7. The beneficiary can choose any implementing agency and that may be different from the agency chosen for first loan.
8. Udyam registration is mandatory.
9. The second loan should lead to additional employment generation.
10. To submit the application for second loan for upgradation the beneficiaries have to apply by filling application form on PMEGP e-portal.

<u>HOW TO APPLY</u>

1. Apply on *https://www.kviconline.gov.in/pmegpeportal/pmegphome*

CREDIT GUARANTEE SCHEME FOR MICRO & SMALL ENTERPRISES (CGTMSE)

OBJECTIVE

1. To encourage first generation entrepreneurs to venture into self employment opportunities by facilitating credit guarantee support for collateral free/third party guarantee free loans to micro and small enterprises (MSEs) especially in the absence of collateral.

KEY BENEFITS

1. Credit guarantee for a loan upto Rs 5 crores , without collateral and third party guarantee.
2. Guarantee coverage ranges from 85% (Micro enterprise upto Rs 5 lakh) to 75% (others)
3. 50% coverage is for retail activity.

SCHEME APPLICABLE FOR

1. Micro and small enterprises.

DETAILED INFORMATION

1. Any collateral and/or third party guarantee free credit facility (both fund based as well as non-fund based) extended by eligible institutions, to new as well as existing micro and small enterprises, including service enterprises, with a maximum credit cap of Rs 2 crores are eligible for guarantee under the scheme. Recently guarantee coverage made eligible to select NBFCs and small finance Banks.
2. The guarantee cover available under the scheme is to the extent of 50%,75%,80% & 85% of the sanctioned amount of the credit facility. The extent of guarantee cover is 85% for micro enterprises for credit upto Rs 5 lakh. The extent of guarantee cover is 50% of the sanctioned amount of the credit facility for credit from Rs 10 lakh to 1 crore per MSE borrower for retail trade activity.
3. The extent of guarantee cover is 80% for (1) Micro and small enterprises operated and/or owned by women and (2) All credits/loans in NER for credit facilities upto Rs 50 lakh. In case of default, the trust settled the claim upto 75% of the amount in default of the credit facility extended by the lending institution for credit facilities upto Rs 2 crore.

HOW TO APPLY

1. Through member lending institution (Bank & NBFCs)
2. For detailed guidelines please visit *https://www.cgtmse.in*

MICRO & SMALL ENTERPRISES CLUSTER DEVELOPMENT PROFRAMME

<u>OBJECTIVE</u>

1. To support the sustainability and growth of MSEs by addressing common issues such as improvement of technology, skills & amp, quality, market access etc.
2. To create upgrade infrastructural facilities in the new/ existing industrial areas/ clusters of MSEs.
3. To set up common facility centres (for testing, training, raw material depot, effluent treatment, complementing production process etc)
4. Promotion of green and sustainable manufacturing technology for clusters.

<u>KEY BENEFITS</u>

1. Creation of common facility centres including plug & play facilities.
2. Support for infrastructure development projects including flatted factory complexes.

<u>SCHEME APPLICABLE FOR</u>

1. Existing entrepreneurs (In form of a special purpose vehicle)

<u>DETAILED INFORMATION</u>

1. Common facility centres – Creation of "tangible assets" such as common production/processing centre, design centres, testing facilities including plug and play facilities. Government assistance upto 80% of maximum project cost of Rs 30 crores.
2. Infrastructure development – Development of land, roads, drainage, power distribution etc, in new/existing industrial (multi-product) areas/estates/flatted factory complex. Government assistance upto 70% of the maximum project cost of Rs 15 crores.

<u>HOW TO APPLY</u>

1. Apply on *https://cluster.dcmsme.gov.in*

ENTREPRENEUR AND SKILL DEVELOPMENT PROGRAMME (ESDP) SCHEME

<u>OBJECTIVE</u>

1. To promote new enterprises, capacity building of existing MSMEs and inculcating entrepreneurial culture in the country

<u>KEY BENEFITS</u>

1. Widen the base of Entrepreneurship by development, achievement, motivation and entrepreneurial skill to the different section of the society.

<u>SCHEME APPLICABLE FOR</u>

1. Aspiring and existing entrepreneurs.

DETAILED INFORMATION

1. Entrepreneurship awareness programme (EAP)- One day training programme is conducted for entrepreneurship/self-employment awareness and motivation to different sections of the society including SC/ST/Women, differently abled, Ex-servicemen and BPL persons as career option.
2. Entrepreneurship cum skill development programme (E-SDP) – Six weeks training programme is conducted for entrepreneurship and skill training in agro-based products, Hosier, food & fruit processing industries, carpet weaving, mechanical engineering workshop/machine shop, heat treatment, electroplating, basic/advance welding/fabrication/sheet metal work, Basic/advance carpentry, glass & ceramics etc.
3. Advance E-SDP: The one-week advance ESDP programs are conducted through IIMs/IITs/ICAR/CSIR/BARC/IISC/NIT/Agricultural university of central and state government etc.
4. -Management development program (MDP) – One week training program for management capacity building training to existing entrepreneurs and their supervisory staff in Industrial management, Human resource management, marketing management, export management/documentation & procedures, material management, financial/working capital management, information technology, digital marketing, quality management/QMS/ISO 9000/EMS, WTO, IPR, supply chain management, retail management, logistic management etc.
5. Advance MDP: The one-week advance MDP training programs are conducted through state administrative training institutes (ATIs) and/or other reputed institutions in this domain of central or state governments/NITs/Regional engineering colleges/Agriculture colleges/autonomous bodies of central/state government to provide MDP training to MSMEs promoters/executives.

HOW TO APPLY

1. Apply on *http://dcmsme.gov.in/Enterprise&skillDevelopment.htm* and *http://msmedi.dcmsme.gov.in*

ASSISTANCE TO TRAINING INSTITUTIONS

The assistance is provided to National level training institutions operating under the ministry of MSME, namely NI-MSME, KVIC, coir board, tool rooms, NSIC & MGIRI in the form of capital grant for the purpose of creation and strengthening of infrastructure and support for entrepreneurship development and skill development training programmes. Assistance is provided to existing state level EDIs i.e. owned and controlled by state government/UT for creation or strengthening/expansion of their training infrastructure.

COIR VIKAS YOJNA (UMBRELLA SCHEME)
OBJECTIVE
1. Coir Vikas Yajna (CVY) is an umbrella scheme being implemented by coir board, for the development of coir industry all over the country. Under this scheme the board is implementing following sub schemes/programmes
2. Science and technology: To modernize of production process, development of machinery and equipment, Product development and diversification, development of environment friendly technologies, technology transfer, Incubation, testing and service facilities etc.
3. -Skill upgradation: With a view to disseminate information on the schemes and latest technologies available in coir sector and also to attract prospective entrepreneurs to this sector, the board organizes entrepreneurship development programmes, workshops, seminars etc.
4. Mahila Coir Yojna: This is a women-oriented self-employment scheme. The scheme is intended to provide training with stipend facilities and creation of self-employment opportunities to rural women artisans
5. The details of the scheme are available in the coir board website – *http://coirboard.gov.in*

PROCUREMENT AND MARKETING SUPPORT (PMS) SCHEME
OBJECTIVE
1. The scheme aim to promote new market access initiatives like organizing/participation in national/international trade fairs/exhibitions/MSME expo etc.

SCHEME COMPONENTS
1. Market access
2. Capacity building
3. Development of retailoutlet

SCHEME APPLICABLE FOR
1. Manufacturing/Service sectors MSEs having valid Udyam registration certificate

APPLY ON
1. *www.dcmsme.gov.in*

INTERNATIONAL COOPERATION SCHEME
OBJECTIVE
1. The scheme aim to build capacity of MSMEs for entering export market by facilitating their participation in international exhibitions/fairs/conferences/seminar/buyer-seller meets abroad as well as providing them with actionable market-intelligence and reimbursement of various costs involved in export of goods and services.

APPLY ON
1. *http://ic.msme.gov.in*

NATIONAL SC/ST HUB SCHEME
OBJECTIVE
1. To provide professional support to schedule cast and schedule tribe entrepreneurs to fulfill the obligations under the central government public procurement policy for micro and small enterprises order 2012, adopt applicable business practices and leverage the stand-up India initiatives.

KEY BENEFITS
1. 25% subsidy on purchase of plant and machinery/equipment or Rs 25 lakh whichever is less.
2. Marketing and mentoring support through participation in exhibitions and vendor development programmes.
3. Reimbursement of fees charged for bank loan processing, testing services, membership of export promotion council, membership in government promoted eCommerce portals, single point registration schemes in NSI.
4. For detailed guideline visit https://www.scsthub.in/

A SCHEME FOR PROMOTION OF INNOVATION, RURAL INDUSTRIES AND ENTREPRENEURSHIP (ASPIRE)
OBJECTIVE
1. To set-up a network of livelihood business incubators (LBIs), predominantly in rural and underserved areas, to promote innovation and accelerate entrepreneurship for the following:-
2. Generate employment opportunities by facilitating formal, scalable micro-enterprise creation in agro-rural sector.
3. Skill, up-skill, re-skill unemployed , self employed/wage earners in new technologies in agro-rural sector.
4. Provide skilled human capital to nearby industrial clusters and promote innovations for strengthening the competitiveness in the MSME sector.

KEY BENEFITS
1. Maximum of 1 crore to government agencies and 75 lakh to private agencies for procuring plant and machinery.
2. Maximum of 1 crore to government and private agencies as operational expenditure support towards manpower cost, running incubation, and skill development programers etc.

SCHEME APPLICABLE FOR
1. Any agency/institution of government of India/state government or existing training centres under ministries/departments of government of India/state government, industry associations, academic institutions.
2. Any not-for-profit private institutions with experience in successfully executing incubation and/or skill development programs may be eligible to set up an LBI.

APPLY ON
1. *https://aspire.msme.gov.in/ASPIRE/AFHome.aspx*

KHADI GRAMODYOG VIKAS YOJNA- UMBRELLA SCHEME

OBJECTIVE

1. To increase productivity and wages of Khadi Artisans
2. To increase infrastructure of Khadi production
3. To increase Khadi production, sales and employment.
4. Development of village industries and increase number of rural artisans.
5. To revive the traditional and inherent skills of rural artisans.
6. To renovate and modernize sales outlets.
7. To promote marketing and export.

KEY BENEFITS

-Khadi Vikas Yojna-

1. Modified market development assistance (MMDA) – Subsidy of 35% on prime cost for cotton/muslin, wool and poly Vastra and 20% on prime cost for silk khadi.
2. Interest subsidy eligibility certificate scheme (ISEC) – Khadi institution is required to pay only 4% interest rate. The difference between the actual interest charged by the bank and 4% is borne by KVIC as "Interest subsidy"
3. Work-shed scheme for Khadi artisans – Individual work-sheds (20 Sq mtrs) Rs 1,20,000 or 75% of the cost of work-shed including toilet whichever is less. Group work-shed (10 sq mtr per artisan) Rs 80,000/- or 75% of the cost of the work-shed including toilet whichever is less.
4. Strengthening infrastructure of existing weak khadi institutions – Financial assistance for revival with ceiling limit of Rs 15 lakh. Financial assistance under marketing infrastructure for renovation of departmental sales outlets of KVIC/KVIB and institutional sales with the ceiling limit of Rs 25 lakh.

-Gramodyog Vikas Yojna-

1. Agarbatti programme under wellness and cosmetic industries (WCI) – Training programme in agarbatti industry. Distribution of pedal operated/automatic agarbatti machinery to trained artisans.
2. Leather footwear activity under handmade paper leather and plastic industry (HMPLPI) – Training on designing and manufacturing of footwear. Distribution of machinery and tool kits to trained artisans.
3. Pottery activity under mineral based industry (MBI) – Training on wheel pottery. Distribution of tools and equipments (Electric potter, wheel, blunger) to trained artisans.
4. Beekeeping activity/Honey mission programme under agro-based & food processing industries (ABFPI) – Bee keeping skill development training. Distribution of 10 bee boxes with live bee colonies and one set of tool kit (containing one knife, smoker, hive tool and bee veil) to trained beneficiaries.
5. Waste wood/Turn woodcraft/wooden toy/products of panchgavya under rural engineering and new technology.

-Training on waste-wood, turn-wood craft, wooden toy and in panchgavya based products. Distribution of tool kit to all trained artisans-

1. Hand made paper and fibre related activities under hand made paper, plastic and leather industry – Training on paper conversion, paper plate and dona (bowl) making, paper mache, fibre extraction and fancy article making and ban making (two ply). Distribution of machinery and tool kits to trained artisans.
2. Agro-food based food processing industries – Training on palm Gur, Tamarind, fruits and vegetables, village oil, spices & condiments, cane and bamboo. Distribution of machinery and tool kits to trained artisans.
3. Service Industry – Training to electricians and plumbers, and digniTEA (Tea vending on bicycle). Distribution of toolkit to trained beneficiaries.

SCHEME APPLICABLE FOR

1. Khadi Institutions (KIs) registered with KVIC or state Khadi and village industries board (KVIB) and Khadi artisans.
2. The beneficiaries may be identified by KVIC, NGOs/Kis/Vis/KVIBs/DICs/FPOs etc.
3. Age group 18-55 years.
4. Having valid Aadhar card or any other identity card issued by Government.
5. One person from one family is eligible for the assistance under KGVY.
6. Persons who have availed benefits from other Government schemes for the same / similar purpose is not eligible.
7. Preference will be given to the people belonging to SC/ST/Women/Unemployed youth/BPL category etc.

HOW TO APPLY

1. Apply on *http://www.kviconline.gov.in*

Some new schemes have also been introduced by ministry of MSME, keeping in view financial assistance to the larger population of micro entrepreneurs and artisans.

Some new schemes have also been introduced by ministry of MSME, keeping in view financial assistance to the larger population of micro entrepreneurs and artisans.

The schemes are as under:

Sr	NAME OF THE SCHEME	FEATURES
1	PM VISWAKARMA-ENABLING ARTISANS AND CRAFTSPEOPLE TO BUILD ENTERPRISES	<u>KEY BENEFITS</u>: 1. PM Viswakarma Certificate and ID card 2. Training for skill upgradation and stipend of Rs 500/- per day. 3. Toolkit up to Rs 15000/- 4. Collateral free loan up to Rs 3 lakh for Viswakarma brothers and sisters. 5. Incentive for digital transaction. 6. Marketing assistance like quality certification, branding , and advertisement for products. 7. 18 type of traditional artisans and crafts people are eligible for enjoying the benefit. <u>HOW TO APPLY</u>: 1. Viswakarma brothers and sisters may visit their nearest CSC.
2	TOOL ROOMS AND TECHNICAL INSTITUTIONS- (A component of Infrastructure development & capacity building)	<u>KEY BENEFITS</u>: 1. Improves access of MSMEs to tooling facilities for enhancement of their efficiency and providing industry ready manpower by conducting training programme. 2. Total 18 MSME tool rooms & technical institutions established Pan India serving in the relevant sector. <u>HOW TO APPLY</u>: 1. Online application can be filled at *http://dcmsme.gov.in/CLCS_TUS_scheme/Tool_Room_Tech_Institutions/Scheme_guidelines.aspx*
3	MSME CHAMPIONS SCHEME	<u>ABOUT THE SCHEME</u> 1. Ministry of MSME had been implementing credit linked capital subsidy and technology upgradation scheme (CLCS-TUS) for promoting competitiveness among MSME. There are 3 components under the Champions scheme, these are : 2. MSME-sustainable zero effect zero defect (ZED) 3. MSME- Innovative for incubation, IPR & design 4. MSME-competitive (Lean) 5. Digital MSME <u>HOW TO APPLY</u>: - Visit *www.zed.msme.gov.in* - Visit *www.innovative.msme.gov.in* - Visit *www.lean.msme.gov.in*

The MSME sector is an important pillar of Indian economy as it contributes greatly to the growth of the nation. Government of India also announced number of other initiatives, to promote MSME sector. The flagship announcements are as under:

ATMANIRBHAR BHARAT ABHIYAN: Under the announcement of Atmanirbhar Bharat in 2020, Government of India made following allocations:

1. Rs 20,000/- crore sub-ordinated debt for stressed MSMEs – This scheme seeks to extend support to the promoter/(s) of the operational MSMEs which are stressed and have become NPA as on 30th April 2020. Promoters of the MSMEs will be given credit equal to 15% of their stake (equity+debt) or Rs 75 lakh, whichever is lower. The maximum tenor of repayment will be 10 years. There will be a moratorium of 7 years on repayment of principal. 90% of guarantee coverage would come with the scheme/trust and remaining 10% from the concerned promoters.
2. Rs 50,000/- crore equity infusion for MSMEs through Fund of Funds – Government of India has created a corpus of Rs 10,000 crore called fund-of funds (FoF). It will provide equity funding to MSMEs having growth potential and viability.
3. The NSIC venture capital fund limited a subsidiary company of NSIC has been incorporated under companies law 2013 for anchoring the funds. The guidelines on self-reliant India (SRI) fund for operationalization of FoF for MSMEs have been issued of 5th August 2020 and it's implementation is progressive.
4. Global tenders to be disallowed upto Rs 200/- crores – Indian MSMEs and other companies have often faced unfair competition from foreign companies. Government of India has announced that global tenders will be disallowed in government procurement upto Rs 200 crore. This will be a step towards self-reliant India and support make in India.
5. New definition of MSMEs – The new MSME definition which is effective from 1st July 2020, focusses on composite criteria of investment and turnover ad is represented in the following table:

Classification	Micro Enterprises	Small Enterprises	Medium Enterprises
Manufacturing Enterprises and Enterprises rendering Services	Investment in Plant and Machinery or Equipment: Not more than Rs.1 crore and Annual Turnover; not more than Rs. 5 crores	Investment in Plant and Machinery or Equipment: Not more than Rs.10 crore and Annual Turnover; not more than Rs. 50 crores	Investment in Plant and Machinery or Equipment: Not more than Rs.50 crore and Annual Turnover; not more than Rs. 250 crores

6. Rs 3 lakh crore collateral-free automatic loans for businesses including MSMEs – Emergency
    credit-line to MSMEs from Banks and NBFCs of 20% of entire outstanding credit as on 29th
    Feb 2020. Following criteria has been laid down:

- Borrowers with up to Rs 25 crore outstanding and Rs 100 crore turnover are eligible.
- Loans to have 4-year tenor with moratorium of 12 months on principal repayment.
- Interest to be capped.
- 100% credit guarantee cover to Banks and NBFCs on principal and interest.
- Scheme can be availed till 31st Oct 2020, with no guarantee fee and no fresh collateral.

START-UP INDIA : The Startup India initiative is closely related to the promotion of MSMEs as it aims to foster a robust startup ecosystem in India. Launched in January 2016, this flagship initiative by the Government of India focuses on supporting entrepreneurs and transforming India into a nation of job creators1. Here are some key aspects of how Startup India is related to MSMEs:

1. Startups recognized under the Startup India initiative can avail various tax benefits, including income tax exemptions for three consecutive years. This helps new businesses, including MSMEs, to grow without the burden of heavy taxes.
2. The "Ease of Doing Business" initiative simplifies the process of starting and running a business by providing self-certification for nine labor laws and environmental laws through the Startup India portal. This reduces the regulatory burden on MSMEs.
3. The Fund of Funds for Startups (FFS) scheme, part of Startup India, provides financial support to startups, including MSMEs, by investing in venture capital funds that in turn invest in startups.
4. Startup India provides market access support through various schemes and platforms, helping MSMEs to expand their reach and connect with potential customers and investors
5. Pradhan Mantri Mudra Yojana (PMMY) launched in 2015 is the scheme which provides financial support to micro-enterprises through various loan products, categorized into Shishu, Kishor, and Tarun, catering to different stages of business development
6. The Skill India Mission focuses on providing skill development training to the workforce in the MSME sector to improve productivity and competitiveness. It includes initiatives like Pradhan Mantri Kaushal Vikas Yojana (PMKVY) and Recognition of Prior Learning (RPL).
7. Startup India Seed Fund Scheme (SISFS) provides financial assistance to startups, including MSMEs, for proof of concept, prototype development, product trials, and market entry.

PM GATI SHAKTI MASTER PLAN - A comprehensive infrastructure development plan aimed at integrating various modes of transport and improving logistics efficiency for MSMEs, reducing costs, and enhancing market access.

MSME SAMBANDH - is an initiative to monitor the procurement by Central Public Sector Enterprises (CPSEs) from MSMEs. This ensures that MSMEs get their fair share of procurement opportunities from government agencies and large corporations.

MSME SAMADHAAN - Is a portal for MSMEs to register complaints regarding delayed payments from buyers. The platform facilitates the resolution of payment issues, ensuring timely payments to MSMEs.

STAND-UP INDIA SCHEME - Is the scheme aims to promote entrepreneurship among women and Scheduled Caste (SC) and Scheduled Tribe (ST) communities by providing bank loans ranging from INR 10 lakh to INR 1 crore for setting up new enterprises.

These additional initiatives further demonstrate the Indian government's commitment to supporting MSMEs through various financial, technological, and infrastructural measures. By addressing the unique challenges faced by MSMEs, these programs help create a conducive environment for their growth and contribute to India's overall economic development.

CHAPTER-7
OPENING BANK ACCOUNT

Opening a bank account is vital step for MSMEs as it provides a foundation for efficient financial management, access to credit, eligibility for government schemes, professional credibility, efficient payroll management, digital transactions, robust record-keeping, and risk management. It is a crucial step towards building a sustainable and successful business.

Bank account helps separate personal and business finances, simplifying accounting and financial management. It allows for the accurate tracking of all business transactions, making it easier to monitor expenses, revenues, and overall financial health.

Banks often require a business bank account to process loan applications. Access to credit is vital for MSMEs to fund their operations, expand, and invest in growth opportunities. A business bank account can help establish the MSME's credit history, improving its chances of securing future loans and credit lines.

Many government schemes and subsidies for MSMEs require a business bank account for direct benefit transfers. This ensures timely and efficient receipt of funds. Having a business bank account is often a prerequisite for availing various government initiatives designed to support MSMEs. A business bank account adds to the professional image of an MSME, enhancing its credibility with clients, suppliers, and partners. It facilitates smooth and professional transactions with clients, enabling them to make payments directly to the business account.

Efficient Payroll Management, Digital Transactions, Record Keeping and Auditing and Risk Management are the most important segment of an enterprise which can easily be controlled by maintaining a business bank account.

Disciplined financial transactions are crucial for MSMEs to maintain financial health and achieve long-term success. Proper financial management ensures that business operations run smoothly, risks are minimized, and opportunities for growth are maximized.

Some points to ponder with respect to business bank account:

- Never use personal account for business transaction. There should be a separate current account preferably by the name and title of the business entity.
- Effort should be taken to maximize and route all business transactions through business account only, and not by and through personal account, because each transaction along with narration of the transaction is being scrutinized by banks to assess loan eligibility; and also, being looked by tax authorities in case of any scrutiny. During audit of the entity, bank statement for a financial year is the most vital document for auditors.

- Separating personal and business finances by maintaining a dedicated business bank account is essential. This helps in accurate tracking of business expenses and revenues, simplifying accounting, and ensuring compliance with tax regulations. Regular monitoring of cash flow is vital to ensure that the business has sufficient liquidity to meet its obligations and invest in growth opportunities.
- Adopting digital payment methods and maintaining detailed financial records enhance transparency and reduce the risk of errors and fraud. Using accounting software can streamline financial reporting and provide real-time insights into the financial performance of the business.
- Timely invoicing and follow-up on payments ensure a steady cash flow and reduce the risk of bad debts. Additionally, budgeting and financial planning enable MSMEs to allocate resources efficiently, set financial goals, and track progress.

Moreover, disciplined financial transactions build credibility with banks, investors, and other stakeholders, facilitating access to credit and investment. In summary, disciplined financial transactions are the foundation for the sustainable growth and success of MSMEs.

When selecting the right bank account, MSMEs should consider nature of business, transaction volume, interest and fees and good banking relationship. Selecting the appropriate bank account is vital for MSMEs to manage their finances effectively. A combination of current accounts for daily transactions, savings accounts for surplus funds, fixed and recurring deposits for investments, and trade and cash credit accounts for specific business needs can provide a comprehensive banking solution. By choosing the right accounts, MSMEs can ensure smooth financial operations, build creditworthiness, and position themselves for sustainable growth and success.

There are following types of account which most of the business entities maintain for day-to-day smooth functioning:
Current Account:
1. A current account is designed to handle a large number of transactions without any limitations, making it suitable for businesses. MSMEs often have a high volume of daily transactions.
2. Many banks offer overdraft facilities with current accounts, allowing MSMEs to withdraw more money than they have in their account, which can help manage short-term liquidity issues.
3. Unlike savings accounts, current accounts typically do not earn interest on the balance, but they offer numerous features that cater to the transactional needs of businesses.
4. In current account there is no cap on the number of transactions, making it ideal for businesses with frequent deposits and withdrawals. Additional services such as cheque books, demand drafts, and online banking facilities are often provided. Maintaining a current account with regular transactions helps build the business's credit history, which can be beneficial for securing loans in the future.

Savings Account:
1. Though not typically used for business transactions, a savings account can help MSMEs earn interest on surplus funds, providing an additional income stream this is why it's important. It can serve as a contingency fund for unexpected expenses or downturns in business.
2. It provides interest on the deposited amount, helping in better fund management acts as a safety net for unforeseen financial requirements.

Fixed Deposit Account:
1. A fixed deposit account is an excellent option for MSMEs to park their surplus funds and earn higher interest compared to savings accounts. It's important because generally it offers higher interest rates than regular savings accounts. Considered a safe investment option with assured returns.
2. To meet exigency fund requirement one can avail Overdraft or term loan facility against Fixed deposits.

Recurring Deposit Account:
1. Recurring deposit is other way of Fixed deposit where fund is deposited on perpetual basis and not in a lump sum basis unlike Fixed deposit.
2. Usually in recurring deposit, funds are parked on monthly basis and there is always a maturity date. Now a days so many banks have started Flexi-recurring account where a minimum amount to be deposited is capped, and one can deposit any amount in multiple of the minimum amount declared.
3. For MSMEs looking to save a specific amount regularly, a recurring deposit account is ideal. Recurring deposit encourages disciplined savings by requiring fixed monthly deposits.

Trade Account:
1. For MSMEs involved in export and import, a trade account is crucial to handle foreign currency transactions and manage trade finances. It facilitates foreign exchange transactions and provides services related to international trade.
2. Banks often offer trade financing options like letters of credit and trade loans through these accounts.

Cash Credit or OD Account:
1. A cash credit or overdraft account is virtually a borrowable account where the entity does not employ their own fund but borrow from Banks or any Fis.
2. This is type of account facility is provided to an entity to meet the fund requirement for working capital gap. Facility is essentially a revolving fund where no particular equated installment is fixed, the interest is charged every month on overdrawn balance and need to be serviced by the beneficiary.

The basic documents required for opening business Bank account are
1. ID proof of promoter/(s)
2. Address proof of promoter/(s)
3. Existence of entity proof with address

Following documents are usually accepted by banks for
- ID proof of promoter/(s) – PAN Copy, Aadhar Copy, Passport copy, Driving license etc.
- Address proof of promoter/(s) – Latest Electricity bill, Telephone bill, Gas connection bill, Passport copy, Bank Statement, Aadhar etc.
- Existence of entity proof with address – Certificate of Incorporation, GST certificate, Certificate under shop & establishment act, Partnership deed or any other certificate issued by competent authority.

Every business entity needs to infuse own capital to kick-start their business. The capital may be in the form of share capital, equity or any sub-ordinated debt. It is advisable that such capital be routed through business accounts only for greater transparency.

CHAPTER-8
SET-UP COST & OPERATIONAL COST

Setup or startup cost is a one-time activity to start a new operation. Setting up and operating an MSME (Micro, Small, and Medium Enterprise) involves several costs that can vary depending on the nature and scale of the business. Setup cost is an essential concept in accounting that plays a crucial role in the financial management of a business.

Set-up cost can be referred to the initial expenses incurred when starting a business or implementing a new process or system. This includes expenses for acquiring infrastructure, purchasing equipment, and setting up initial operational processes. For instance, when starting a manufacturing business, setup costs would encompass everything from procuring machinery and raw materials to initial labor expenses.

Start-up or set-up cost can be broadly understood with following major activities:

Registration and Licensing Fees:
1. Udyam Registration: Udyam Registration is the official registration process for MSMEs, which is free of cost and paperless. It provides recognition to the business and eligibility for various government schemes and benefits.
2. Other Licenses: Depending on the type of business and location, additional licenses and permits may be required, such as trade licenses, GST registration, environmental clearances, and more. The costs for these licenses can vary.

Office Space and Utilities:
1. Rent: Renting office or workshop space is a significant setup cost. The rent can vary based on location, size, and facilities. Urban areas typically have higher rental costs compared to rural areas.
2. Utilities: Setting up utilities such as electricity, water, internet, and telephone connections is essential. The initial installation and deposit fees for these services add to the setup costs.

Equipment and Machinery:
1. Purchase or Lease: The cost of purchasing or leasing equipment and machinery depends on the industry and the specific needs of the business. For example, a manufacturing unit may require expensive machinery, while a service-based business may need computers and office equipment.
2. Installation and Setup: Additional costs may be incurred for the installation and setup of machinery and equipment.

Initial Inventory:
1. Raw Materials: Acquiring the initial stock of raw materials or products is crucial for starting operations. The cost will depend on the nature of the business and the quantity of inventory required.

Technology and Software:
1. Accounting Software: Investing in accounting and management software is essential for keeping track of financial transactions and maintaining records.
2. Other Software: Depending on the business, additional software may be required for operations, such as customer relationship management (CRM) systems, point-of-sale (POS) systems, and more.

Marketing and Branding:
1. Logo and Branding: Creating a professional logo and branding materials such as business cards, letterheads, and packaging is important for establishing a brand identity.
2. Marketing Campaigns: Initial marketing efforts, including online advertising, social media campaigns, and promotional materials, are necessary to create awareness and attract customers.

Salaries and Wages:
1. Employee Salaries: Paying monthly salaries to employees is one of the significant operational costs. The salary expenses will depend on the number of employees and their respective roles.
2. Contractor Fees: Fees for any outsourced services or contractors, such as marketing agencies, IT support, and legal services.

Raw Materials and Supplies:
1. Ongoing Inventory: Regular replenishment of raw materials and supplies is essential for continuous production and operations. The cost will vary based on consumption rates and market prices.

Utilities and Maintenance:
1. Ongoing Utilities: Monthly expenses for electricity, water, internet, and other utilities required for day-to-day operations.
2. Maintenance: Regular maintenance of equipment, machinery, and office space to ensure smooth functioning and prevent breakdowns.

Marketing and Advertising:
1. Ongoing Marketing: Continuous marketing efforts, including digital marketing, print ads, and promotional activities, to maintain and grow the customer base.

Insurance:
1. Business Insurance: Insurance coverage for various risks, such as property damage, liability, employee health, and more, is essential for protecting the business.

Loan Repayments:
1. Interest and Principal: Monthly repayments for any business loans taken to finance the setup and growth of the business.

Miscellaneous Expenses:
1. Travel and Transportation: Costs for business travel, transportation of goods, and logistics.
2. Training and Development: Expenses for employee training and development programs to enhance skills and productivity.

The calculation of setup cost involves a meticulous process of estimating capital expenditures and allocating costs for the initial setup of business operations or new projects. This process typically begins with a detailed assessment of the required resources and materials needed for the initiation of the project. The components of setup cost encompass both direct costs, such as specific materials and labor, and indirect costs, which include ongoing expenses and the overall cost structure within the realm of business operations.

Direct costs typically involve clearly identifiable expenses directly attributable to the installation or creation of a new process or system, such as equipment and labor.

On the other hand, indirect costs, like administrative overhead and utilities, may not be as straightforward to allocate but still significantly impact the overall cost structure. Understanding the breakdown of these costs is crucial in managing financial resources effectively and optimizing operational efficiency within a business.

As per generally accepted accounting principles (GAAP) the organizational costs up to certain limitation can be capitalized and amortized in future years for tax purposes.

CHAPTER-9
IMPORTANT MANPOWER RESOURCES

Starting an enterprise is an exciting journey! Hiring the right manpower is crucial for success. A comprehensive understanding of the key roles is required, to start an enterprise. Each role is vital to ensure that different aspects of the business are well-managed and aligned with overall goals.

Some important spread of Manpower allocation can be explained in following manner:

TOP EXECUTIVE: The key person who has conceptualized running the enterprise usually are the Top executive/(s). They usually carry the responsibilities of being
1. Visionary strategist & leader
2. Have power of taking important decisions
3. Have power to handle critical issues in crises as they surface.
4. Have ability to remain steadfast and motivated through challenges.
5. Should act as the main point of contact with Board of Directors, investors and partners.
6. Should have good and effective communication skill in conveying ideas and motivating teams.

TOP MANAGEMENT: The person having expertise in niche segment are usually appointed in respective fields of their expertise. Such positions are mainly:
1. CTO (Chief technology officer)- Should have deep understanding of technology and industry trends. They have the ability to manage multiple projects and deadlines. Carries creative problem-solving and innovative thinking. Works well with other departments to align technology with business goals. Setting technological vision and roadmap, keeping the enterprise on cutting edge of technology, managing and mentoring the tech team, security of technology system and data are the key areas where CTO works.
2. CFO (Chief Financial officer)- Should have in-depth knowledge of finance, accounting and economics. CFO should have the ability of financial planning with business goals, meticulous in financial reporting and analysis, strong analytical and problem-solving abilities, prepare financial statement and reports for stakeholders, managing budget preparation etc.
3. COO (Chief operating officer)- The responsibility of COO is to ensure smooth daily operation, oversees human resources and ensures productive work environment. COO should have the capability to manage administrative functions and logistics, tracks performance metrics and operational KPIs.

SENIOR MANAGEMENT: The senior management positions are created in a gradual manner depending upon the growth in network of enterprise, business volume and mid/lower-level manpower requirement. The priority-wise senior management positions can be created in following manner:
1. Human Resource Manager
2. Marketing Manager
3. Sales Manager
4. Product Manager
5. Customer support Lead
6. Operation Manager
7. Legal Advisor
8. Administrative assistant

These roles mentioned above can provide a strong foundation for any enterprise, ensuring that all critical aspects of the business are managed effectively. As business grows, one can expand team with more specialized roles to support further growth and development.

CHAPTER-10
FINANCIAL RESOURCES

Proper financial resource management is crucial for an enterprise's success and sustainability. It encompasses the strategic planning, organizing, and controlling of financial activities to achieve the organization's goals. Here are several reasons why it is essential:

Ensuring Liquidity: An enterprise must maintain sufficient liquidity to meet its short-term obligations and operational needs. Proper financial management helps ensure that there is enough cash flow to cover expenses such as salaries, rent, and utilities. Without adequate liquidity, a business may face insolvency or bankruptcy.

Facilitating Growth and Expansion: Sound financial resource management enables a business to invest in growth opportunities and expand its operations. This could involve funding for research and development, purchasing new equipment, or entering new markets. Access to financial resources allows a business to innovate and stay competitive in the industry.

Risk Management: Effective financial management involves identifying, assessing, and mitigating financial risks. This includes managing debt levels, diversifying investments, and implementing strategies to protect against market fluctuations. By minimizing risks, a business can safeguard its assets and ensure long-term stability.

Improving Profitability: Proper financial resource management helps optimize the use of resources, leading to cost savings and increased profitability. By carefully monitoring expenses and implementing cost-effective measures, a business can enhance its bottom line. Additionally, efficient financial management allows for better pricing strategies and revenue optimization.

Enhancing Stakeholder Confidence: Investors, creditors, and other stakeholders are more likely to trust and support a business with strong financial management practices. Transparency and accountability in financial reporting build confidence and attract potential investors. This, in turn, provides access to additional capital and growth opportunities.

Compliance and Legal Requirements: Adhering to financial regulations and legal requirements is essential for any business. Proper financial management ensures compliance with tax laws, corporate governance standards, and industry-specific regulations. Non-compliance can result in fines, legal actions, and damage to the company's reputation.

Strategic Decision-Making: Accurate financial information is crucial for making informed business decisions. Proper financial management provides insights into the company's financial health, performance, and future prospects. This enables management to make strategic decisions regarding investments, mergers, acquisitions, and other critical aspects of the business.

Sustainable Operations: Long-term sustainability depends on effective financial planning and management. This includes budgeting, forecasting, and managing resources to ensure that the business can withstand economic downturns and continue to operate successfully.

Financial resources are the backbone of any enterprise, and they can come from a variety of sources. Here are some of the most common sources of financial resources for an enterprise. Each source of financial resource has its own advantages and disadvantages, and businesses often use a combination of these sources to meet their financial needs. Choosing the right mix depends on factors such as the business's size, stage of development, industry, and specific financial goals.

Personal Savings: Many entrepreneurs use their personal savings as initial capital to start their businesses. This source is often the most accessible and requires no formal application process. However, it comes with the risk of losing personal funds if the business does not succeed.

Family and Friends: This informal source of financing involves borrowing money from relatives or friends. The terms are usually flexible, and the interest rates are often lower compared to traditional loans. However, mixing personal relationships with business can sometimes lead to conflicts.

Equity Financing: Equity financing involves selling shares of the company to investors in exchange for capital. Here are some common types:
- Angel Investors: High-net-worth individuals who provide capital to startups in exchange for ownership equity or convertible debt.
- Venture Capitalists: Firms that invest in high-growth potential startups in return for equity. They often provide mentorship and strategic guidance.
- Private Equity Firms: Firms that invest in established businesses requiring capital for expansion or restructuring.

Debt Financing: Debt financing involves borrowing money that must be repaid with interest. Common forms include
- Bank Loans: Traditional loans from banks with fixed or variable interest rates. These loans require collateral and a strong credit history.
- Lines of Credit: Flexible borrowing options that allow businesses to draw funds up to a specified limit as needed and pay interest on the borrowed amount.
- Bonds: Debt securities issued by corporations to raise capital, typically for large projects or expansions. Investors receive periodic interest payments and the principal amount at maturity.
- Trade Credit: Suppliers may extend credit terms to businesses, allowing them to purchase goods or services and pay for them at a later date. This helps manage cash flow and reduce the need for immediate cash outlays.
- Government Grants and Subsidies: Governments offer various grants, subsidies, and tax incentives to support businesses, especially in sectors like technology, renewable energy, and healthcare. These funds do not need to be repaid but often come with specific conditions and reporting requirements.
- Crowdfunding: Crowdfunding platforms like Kickstarter, Indiegogo, and GoFundMe allow businesses to raise small amounts of money from a large number of people. This method can also help validate the business idea and build a customer base before the product or service is launched.
- Retained Earnings: Profits generated by the business can be reinvested to fund operations, expansion, and other growth initiatives. Retained earnings are a sustainable source of funding that does not involve borrowing or diluting ownership.

- Strategic Partnerships and Joint Ventures: Collaborating with other businesses through partnerships or joint ventures can provide access to additional capital, resources, and expertise. These alliances can help share risks and costs associated with new projects or market expansions.
- Leasing: Leasing involves renting assets such as equipment, vehicles, or real estate instead of purchasing them outright. This reduces the initial capital expenditure and allows for better cash flow management. Leasing arrangements can also provide tax benefits and flexibility.
- Invoice Financing: Invoice financing, also known as factoring, allows businesses to obtain immediate cash by selling their unpaid invoices to a third party at a discount. This provides quick access to funds without waiting for customers to pay their invoices.

The ultimate success of an enterprise depends upon the availability of sufficient finance. In other words, finance is the prerequisite for mobilizing the resources of an enterprise. An enterprise requires finance at every stage of its life cycle. For example, in the inception stage, it needs finance for setting up plant and purchasing fixed assets, such as machines and equipment. However, in the development stage, finance is required for continuous mobilization and up gradation of enterprises to survive and grow in today's competitive business environment. In addition, the efficient functioning of various departments, such as production, marketing, research and development, of the enterprise depends on smooth flow of finance. For example, the marketing department of an enterprise needs a sufficient amount of funds for promoting and distributing the product. Therefore, an enterprise needs to be prudent while managing finance for a project. The financial needs of an enterprise depend on various factors, such as size and nature of the business.

An enterprise can raise long term finance by issuing equity and preference shares, borrowing capital and using retained earnings. On the other hand, medium term finance can be raised through lease finance, hire purchase and public deposits. Short term finance is raised through trade credit, installment credit, certificates of deposits and bank loans. Apart from this, an enterprise can also raise finance from various financial agencies such as commercial banks and co-operative banks. The Indian government has opened several institutions such as Small Industries Development Bank of India (SIDBI) and National Small Industries Corporation Ltd (NSIC), to provide financial assistance to small and medium scale entrepreneurs.

Programs like the Startup India Seed Fund Scheme provide grants and convertible debentures to help MSMEs with prototype development, market research, and hiring skilled staff. Starting and growing a Micro, Small and Medium Enterprise (MSME) can be challenging. Often, these businesses struggle to secure the initial funding they need to transform their ideas into reality. This is where the Startup India Seed Funding Scheme comes in as a game-changer. The Indian government launched this program with the express purpose of providing MSMEs with critical early-stage capital, commonly referred to as MSME seed funding.

Through the provision of financial support, the Startup India Seed Funding Scheme enables MSMEs to bring their creative concepts to market. This may entail financing the creation of prototypes, market research, the employment of qualified staff, or even the expansion of manufacturing facilities. With this crucial assistance, MSMEs may get past the early growth obstacles and develop into prosperous companies that will add to the Indian economy by generating jobs.

There are basically two stages of financing an organization: (1) Early-Stage Financing (2) Later Stage Financing.

Early-stage financing can be categorized in following stages -
1. Seed Capital stage
2. Start-up stage
3. Second round financing

And later stage financing can be categorized in following stages-
1. Expansion finance
2. Bridge financing
3. Replacement financing
4. Turnaround financing
5. Buyout deals
6. Management buyouts
7. Management buy-ins

Every enterprise requires finance for establishing its business and carrying out various related activities. Financing a new enterprise essentially involves two parts, viz, estimating the funds/capital requirement and deciding sources. An enterprise has two types of financial requirements, namely, fixed capital and working capital, which are discussed as follows:

1. **Working Capital**: It is that capital which is invested in current or short-term assets. It covers expenses, such as buying the raw material, payment of wages and salaries, rent, fuel, electricity and water, repairs and maintenance and advertising. The prepaid expenses, cash, inventory and the bills receivable are regarded as current assets. The funds invested in current assets are recovered by realizing cash. Therefore, working capital is also regarded as revolving capital or circulating capital.
2. **Fixed Capital**: The fixed capital helps in purchasing fixed or durable assets, such as land, building, machinery, equipment and furniture. The fixed capital is also known as long term capital. The amount of fixed capital depends mainly upon the nature and size of the business. The manufacturing industries requires huge amount of investment whereas the trading concerns require comparatively lesser investments.

An enterprise can raise funds only, if it is clearly determining its financial requirements. Estimating the financial requirements for an enterprise involves determining the total amount of capital required for various needs of the business and deciding the sources and methods to raise it. The financial needs can be fulfilled though the owned capital or the borrowed capital. The financial requirements on the basis of period of use are classified into three types, which are as follows:

- **Long-Term Capital**: Long term capital is required to finance the fixed capital and permanent part of the working capital. It is raised through various sources, such as by issuing debentures and shares and taking loans and advances from banks and financial institutions. It is the capital which is required for a period of five years or more.

- **Medium-Term Capital**: This kind of capital is required for performing different activities viz. renovation of buildings, expenditure on advertising and modernization of machinery. This capital can be raised from different sources such as issuing of debentures and shares and reinvestment of accumulated profits. The medium-term capital is required for a period of two to five years.
- **Short-Term Capital**: Short term capital is required to finance the current assets and to meet day-to-day expenses. It can be raised from various sources such as banks, installment credit and trade credit. The short-term capital is needed for a period of less than a year.

MSME sectors are being offered good scope for Bank finance through its diversified base, backward and forward linkages with other sectors.

Credit facilities extended by Banks and financial Institutions can be classified into two broad categories viz Fund based & non-fund based. However, there are certain type of advances which do not involve deployment of funds at least at the initial stage though in contingencies funds are also involved. Such facilities are called non-fund based.

Most of the established Banks and financial institutions have adopted a centralized credit processing system for appraisal of loan application, these are commonly called Central loan processing cell or CLPC. These CLPCs are established with specialized officers having sound knowledge of latest IT platforms. The CLPCs comprises of huge database and information of borrowers, their past credit records, banking transactions etc. The branches are mostly functioning as front-line access for common people to approach for loans and advances.

The credit processing for MSMEs mostly undergoes in following 6 stages.

Management Appraisal – Management appraisal is nothing but appraising of the promoters behind the enterprise. The appraisal involves assessment of following parameters:

- The entrepreneur
- The promoter/(s) or Board of Directors
- The chief executive
- The departmental heads.

As per thumb rule of Banking and credit it is said that Management appraisal is the study of following four characteristics commonly known **4Cs**

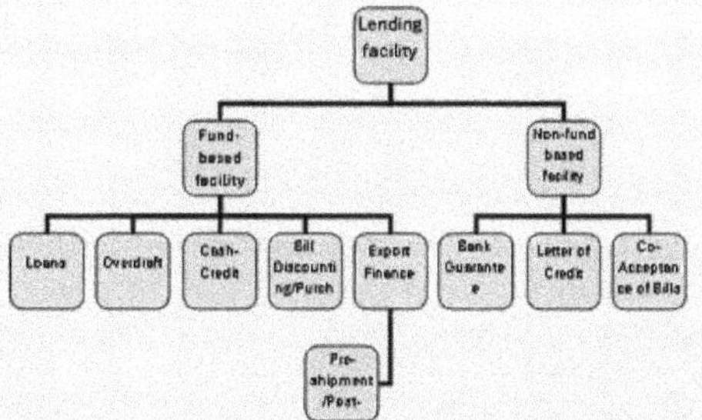

- **Character**: It is the character of the borrower which reflects intention to repay loan. These are honesty, integrity and commitments.

- **Capacity to repay**: Educational, technical and professional qualifications, antecedent, present activity, hands on experience in the line of business, family background, processing special skills or knowledge are the important points which is studied to understand capacity to repay.
- **Capital infused**: A borrower should have some stake in the business so that there exists a consistent interest and excitement for the growth of enterprise. It also gives an input about the ability of the borrower to bail out of the venture in case of adverse scenario.

- **Collateral security**: It is about securities offered to mitigate the risk of default in repayment. Collateral security helps as second line of defense.

Interviewing the borrower, inspection survey, compliance of KYC etc. are part of Management appraisal.

Technical Appraisal: The technical appraisal of a credit proposal involves a detailed study of:

- Availability of basic infrastructure viz Land & building, power, water, electricity etc.
- Plant & Machinery
- Type of products
- Licensing/registration requirement
- Production capacity/manufacturing process
- Raw material
- Labour
- Technology and manufacturing process
- Storage facilities
- Marketing arrangement
- Effluent disposal
- Implementation schedule
- Contingencies.

.Financial Appraisal: Financial appraisal refers to the study of following points:

- Analysis of past working results in case of existing concern.
- Assessment of cost of project.
- Assessment of source of funds/uses of funds
- Balance sheet and ratio analysis.
- Profitability estimates.
- Break-even analysis
- Funds flow and cash flow projections.

Economical Appraisal: While apprising a project it is also seen whether the project is fulfilling priority sector guidelines or non-priority sector guidelines. Whether the project is significantly contributing for the development of the sector and the economy as a whole. Following points are studied in economic appraisal.

- Sensitivity analysis
- Internal rate of return
- Net present value

Market/Environmental appraisal : In order to make proper appraisal of the demand forecasts made by the MSME unit; information such as demand, supply , distribution , pricing and external forces are minutely studied. Some of the methods which are commonly used for forecasting aggregate demand are :-

- Import substitution
- Past trend method
- End-use method
- Correlation and regression method
- Export market

By using above methods general market prospect of the product, its competition, size of the market and share of the proposed unit, price structure, availability of raw material, marketing strategy etc. are evaluated.

Assessment of Loans: Banks/FIs conduct financial statement analysis meticulously when assessing term loan applications to evaluate a borrower's financial health, stability, and repayment capacity. Here's how they typically go about it:-
- Profitability Analysis: They examine the income statement to assess the borrower's ability to generate profits over time. Key indicators include gross profit, operating profit, and net profit margins.
- Liquidity Analysis: By studying the balance sheet, banks check if the borrower has sufficient short-term assets to cover their short-term liabilities. Ratios like the current ratio and quick ratio are commonly used.
- Solvency Analysis: To evaluate the long-term financial stability of the borrower, banks analyze metrics such as debt-to-equity ratio and interest coverage ratio. These help determine the borrower's ability to sustain and repay long-term debts.
- Cash Flow Analysis: Banks pay close attention to the cash flow statement to understand how cash is being generated and utilized. Positive and stable cash flow is a key indicator of the borrower's capacity to meet loan repayment schedules.
- Trend Analysis: They review historical financial data to identify trends in revenue, expenses, and profits. This helps predict future financial performance and assess the growth potential of the business.
- Comparative Analysis: Banks may compare the borrower's financial performance with industry standards or similar businesses to assess competitiveness and stability.

Assessment of Contingent Liabilities: Banks evaluate any off-balance sheet liabilities, such as guarantees or pending legal obligations, which might pose risks to the borrower's financial stability.

By analyzing these aspects, banks form a comprehensive picture of the borrower's financial situation, helping them make informed decisions about approving the term loan.

The commonly used methods for **assessment of working capital finance** are as under: -
- Turnover Method (or Nayak Committee Norms): Under this method, working capital requirements are calculated as a percentage of the business's projected annual turnover. Typically, banks provide 20% of the turnover as working capital, with 5% funded by the borrower and 15% by the bank.
- Cash Flow Method: This method evaluates the cash inflows and outflows of the business to determine the liquidity gap. It focuses on the cash cycle and ensures that sufficient working capital is provided to bridge the shortfall.
- Current Asset-Based Method: In this approach, working capital is assessed based on the current assets of the business, such as inventory, receivables, and cash. Banks typically fund up to a certain percentage of these assets, after deducting current liabilities.
- Operating Cycle Method: This method examines the business's operating cycle, which is the time taken to convert raw materials into finished goods, sell them, and collect payments. The longer the cycle, the higher the working capital requirement.
- Gross Working Capital Method: This approach considers the total current assets of the business, including inventory, debtors, and cash, to determine the working capital requirement.
- Net Working Capital Method: Under this method, the difference between current assets and current liabilities (net working capital) is analyzed to decide the funding needed.
- Projection-Based Method: In this method, banks assess the projected financial statements and business growth plans to estimate the future working capital needs.

These methods enable banks to customize working capital finance solutions based on the specific needs and nature of the business.

CHAPTER-11
RISK ASSESSMENT

Risk assessment in Micro, Small, and Medium Enterprises (MSMEs) is crucial for identifying potential challenges and ensuring business sustainability. MSMEs often face unique risks due to their size, limited resources, and market dynamics. Here's an overview of the key aspects of risk assessment in this sector.

MSMEs are exposed to various risks, including financial, operational, market, and compliance risks. Financial risks arise from inadequate cash flow, high debt levels, or limited access to credit. Operational risks may include supply chain disruptions, equipment failures, or workforce issues. Market risks stem from changing consumer preferences, competition, or economic downturns. Compliance risks involve adhering to legal and regulatory requirements.

The risk assessment process begins with identifying and categorizing potential risks based on their likelihood and impact. This involves analyzing historical data, industry trends, and the specific business environment. Once risks are identified, their impact on the business is evaluated, considering factors such as financial loss, reputational damage, or operational disruptions.

MSMEs must also assess their vulnerabilities and existing risk management measures. This includes reviewing internal controls, insurance coverage, and contingency plans. Based on this analysis, businesses can develop risk mitigation strategies, such as diversifying suppliers, improving financial management, or investing in technology.

Regular monitoring and review of risks are essential to adapt to changing circumstances. MSMEs can benefit from leveraging technology, such as risk management software, to streamline the assessment process and enhance decision-making.

Effective risk assessment enables MSMEs to proactively address challenges, improve resilience, and seize growth opportunities. By fostering a culture of risk awareness, MSMEs can build a strong foundation for long-term success.

Measuring risks in MSMEs involves a systematic approach to quantify their likelihood and potential impact. Here's how different types of risks can be assessed:

- **Financial Risk**: Measured using financial ratios such as debt-to-equity, current ratio, and interest coverage ratio. Analyzing cash flow statements and profitability trends also helps evaluate the financial stability of the business.
- **Operational Risk**: Performance metrics like downtime rates, defect percentages, or supply chain efficiency are used. Conducting regular audits and analyzing operational data help identify vulnerabilities in processes.
- **Market Risk**: Assessed by studying market trends, customer demand patterns, and competitor analysis. Tools like SWOT analysis (Strengths, Weaknesses, Opportunities, Threats) and market surveys can provide valuable insights.

- **Compliance Risk**: Measured by evaluating adherence to regulations, labor laws, and tax policies. Regular compliance checks and audits help ensure all legal requirements are met.
- **Credit Risk**: Calculated through credit scoring models, evaluating the payment history, creditworthiness of customers, and the aging of receivables. This ensures the business can manage its debts and collections effectively.
- **Reputational Risk**: Monitored using social media sentiment analysis, customer feedback, and survey results to gauge public perception of the business.
- **Environmental Risk**: If applicable, assessed by identifying the environmental impact of the business operations through tools like carbon footprint analysis and regulatory compliance.

Quantitative tools like risk assessment matrices (likelihood vs. impact) and qualitative methods like expert judgment or brainstorming sessions can also help in evaluating risks holistically. Tracking these risks regularly allows MSMEs to mitigate them proactively and maintain resilience.

Risk mitigation in MSMEs involves strategies to identify, reduce, and manage potential risks that could disrupt operations or impact profitability. Here are some common methods used:

- **Diversification**: MSMEs can reduce market and operational risks by diversifying their product portfolio, suppliers, and markets. This prevents overdependence on a single source or customer.
- **Insurance**: Purchasing suitable insurance policies for assets, operations, and personnel helps manage financial risks caused by unforeseen events such as accidents, natural disasters, or theft.
- **Financial Planning**: Maintaining proper financial records, cash reserves, and working capital ensures liquidity and reduces the risk of financial instability. Regular audits and ratio analysis enhance financial health.
- **Supplier and Vendor Management**: MSMEs can mitigate supply chain risks by building strong relationships with multiple suppliers and ensuring contracts include contingency clauses for delays or disruptions.
- **Compliance Monitoring**: Regularly reviewing legal and regulatory requirements protects MSMEs from fines or penalties, reducing compliance risks.
- **Technology Adoption**: Using advanced technology for operations, data management, and market research minimizes operational inefficiencies and improves decision-making.
- **Customer Relationship Management**: Building strong relationships with customers and ensuring timely feedback helps reduce market risks due to changing preferences or competition.
- **Contingency Planning**: Preparing for unforeseen events through detailed contingency plans ensures the business can recover quickly from disruptions.
- **Risk Assessment Tools**: MSMEs can use tools such as risk matrices, sensitivity analyses, and forecasting models to identify and address risks proactively.

By implementing these measures, MSMEs can enhance their resilience, maintain stability, and seize growth opportunities despite uncertainties.

Annexure-1

PROJECT PROFILE ON READY TO USE AND THROW UTENSIL MAKINGS FROM SAL AND BANANA LEAF

Table of Contents

INTRODUCTION

In the past mainly rural Indians used ready to use plates and cups for serving foods. These are commonly used for serving food at marriages, religions and social functions. Those cups and plates are made of leaves like Sal, Banana, Butea, arecanut sheath, lotus, palm, etc. with the help of traditional and manual techniques. Now this laborious craft is converted to machine made production with the help of machineries. The machine made technique gives the cups and plates identical and elegant shapes. These cups and plates are bi-degradable, hygienic and less expensive. This craft has huge market potential and it generates employment for the rural people.

PRODUCTS AND ITS APPLICATION

- These cups and plates widely used in the social events like marriages, parties, and religious places to distribute *prasad* and mass feeding.
- There is huge demand of those ready to use and throw utensils in the fast food restaurants, star-hotels.
- Hawkers are also use those extensively.

DESIRED QUALIFICATION FOR PROMOTER

No specific degree require for making those ready to use utensils.

INDUSTRY OUTLOOK/TREND

Ready to use and throw utensils like plastic cutlery, which is a by-product of petroleum, contains several neuro-toxins and carcinogens. These toxins slowly enter the human body. The cutlery manufactured with bio-degradable leaves have no side effect. These plates act as the best alternative for plastics and because of this reason it has a good market in international market. This cottage industry has huge potential, as these products are eco-friendly and less expensive. These products have a good market in Maharashtra, Delhi, Madhya Pradesh and Tamil Nadu. Now more and more people are adopting those products in various functions. There is no pollution control associated with those. India also exported these items to countries like USA, UK, Germany, Australia and other European countries. (HS Code: 4062) is give below:

Year	Export Value (INR Lakh)
2018-2019	10917.39
2019-2020	15349.18
2020-2021	11011.93

MARKET POTENTIAL AND MARKETING ISSUES, IF ANY

As these products are eco-friendly products, there is no marketing issues of these products. Other qualities of these products are:

- No chop down of trees, fallen leaves are collected and turned to value added products.
- Waste to wealth concept.
- No Chemicals, bleaching, PE (Poly Ethylene) coating, Wax coating at any stage.
- Lightweight, sturdy and non-crushable.
- Microwave & Refrigerator safe.
- Holds liquid items for 4 hours without leakage.
- Good for hot, wet and cool food items.

BASIS AND PRESUMPTIONS

- The unit will work for 300 days per annum on a single shift basis.
- The unit can achieve its full capacity utilization during the first month of operation.
- The wages for skilled workers are taken as per prevailing rates in this type of industry.
- Interest rate for total capital investment is calculated @ 10% per annum.
- The entrepreneur is expected to raise 20-25% of the capital as margin money.
- The unit would construct its own building.
- Costs of machinery and equipment are based on average prices of machinery manufacturers.

RAW MATERIAL REQUIREMENTS

Leaves	1.40 lakh
Packing materials	0.10 lakh

MANUFACTURING PROCESS

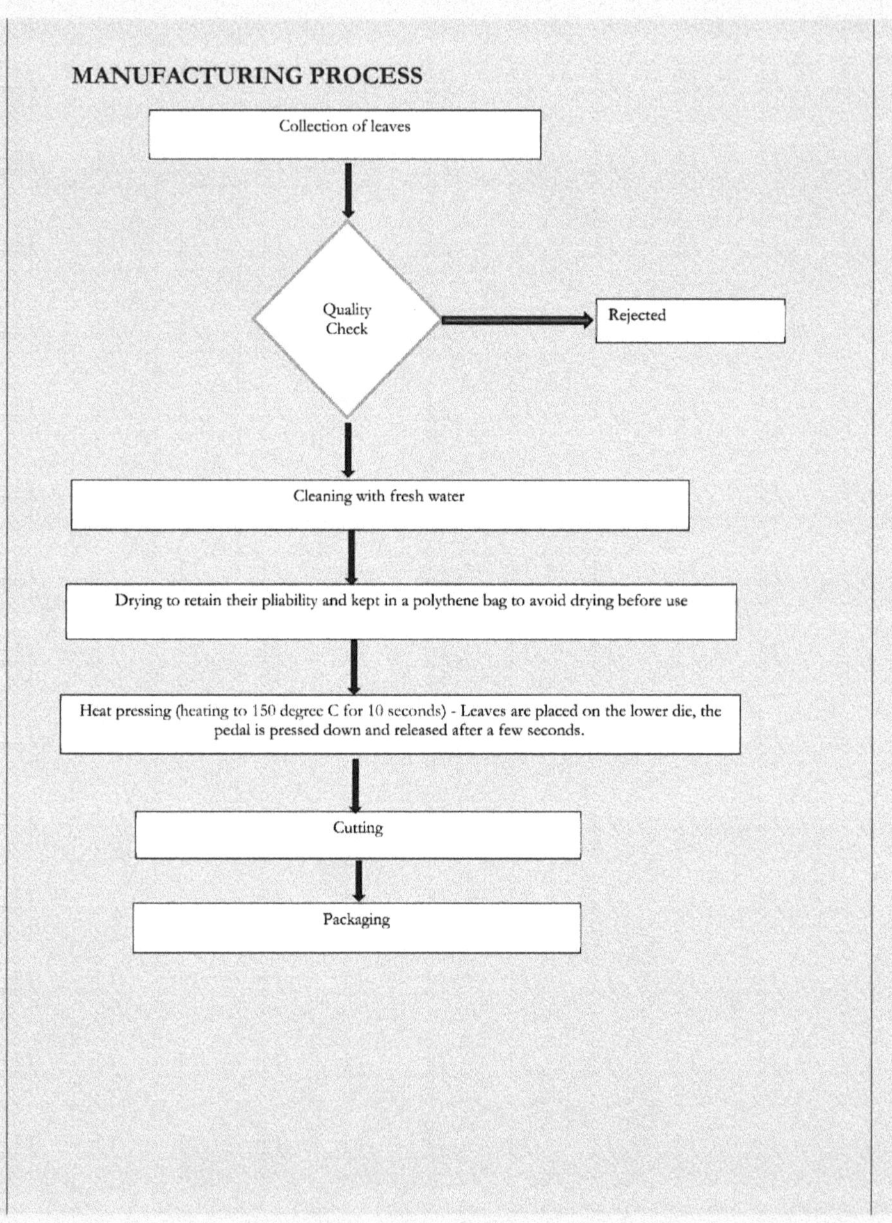

MANPOWER REQUIREMENT (PER MONTH)

Plants

Type	Number	Cost (Rs.)
Owner or entrepreneur	1	20,000
Labour (unskilled)	5	40,000
Total per month		**60,000**

LAND

Particulars	Units	Total Area	Total rent (INR)
Land & building (rent)	Sq. Mt.	100	10000

MACHINERY SPECIFICATIONS

Types of machinery	Quantity	Price (INR Lakh)
Leaf cup and plate making machine lever on bearings - 3	3	1.00
Dies with circular dia - 4	4	0.40
Die square katori - 3	3	0.40
Blow lamp with fittings attachment 1	1	0.05
Tool kit - 1	1	0.05
Total		1.90
Erection and electrification @ 10% of machinery cost		0.20
Office furniture & fixtures		0.40
Total*		**2.50**

* Cost of the machine is exclusive of GST & other than transportation cost.

UTILITIES (per month)

Sl. No	Particulars	Cost (Rs. Lakh)
1	Electricity (Single phase) 3 HP	**0.03**

Other Contingent Expenses

Particulars	Amount (Rs. lakh)
Repairs and maintenance @10%	0.20
Consumables & spares Transport & Travel Publicity Postage & stationery Telephone	0.12
Insurance	0.03
Total	0.35

WORKING CAPITAL ASSESSMENT (per month)

Sl. No	Particulars	Cost (Rs. Lakh)
1	Manpower	0.60
2	Raw materials	0.13
3	Utilities	0.03
4	Other contingent expenses	0.35
	Working Capital	1.11
	Working Capital for 3 months	3.33 (rounded to 3.30 lakhs)

COST OF THE PROJECT

Sl. No	Particulars	Cost (Rs. Lakh)
1	Land & building rent	1.20
2	Plant & Machinery	2.50
3	Contingencies @2% of the project	0.10
5	Pre-operative cost	0.50
	Total	**4.70**
	Loan Amount 75%	**3.525**

CAPITAL INVESTMENT

Sl. No	Particulars	Cost (Rs. Lakh)
1	Land	1.20
2	Plant & Machinery and Furniture	2.50
3	Preoperative Expenses	0.50
	Total Fixed Capital	4.20
4	Working Capital (for 3 months)	3.30
	Total	**7.50**

IMPLEMENTATION SCHEDULE

Project Stages	Months...			
	1	2	3	4
Acquisition of Land				
Ordering of Machinery				
Delivery of Machinery				
Term/Wkg Loan Sanction				
Installation of Machinery				
Commissioning of Plant				
RM/Inputs Procurement				
Manpower Appointments				

Commercial Production				

SALES REVENUE

Particulars	Rate per 100 pack (INR)	1st year	2nd year	3rd year	4th year	5th year
Total Capacity: leaf plates 6 lakh (assorted)**, leaf cups 10 lakh** (assorted)						
Capacity Utilization	-	70%	80%	90%	90%	90%
Production of leaf plates (in lakh)		4.2	4.8	5.4	5.4	5.4
Production of leaf cups		7	8	9	9	9
Rate of leaf plates (per 100 pieces) INR		300	320	340	360	370
Rate of leaf cups (per 100 pieces) INR		50	60	70	80	90
Revenue from sales of plates (INR Lakhs)		12.6	15.36	18.36	19.44	19.98
Revenue from sales of cups (INR Lakhs)		3.5	4.8	6.3	7.2	8.1
Total Revenue from sales		16.1	20.16	24.66	26.64	28.08

PROFITABILITY CALCULATION

Sl. No.	Particulars	Rate per 100 (INR)	1st year	2nd year	3rd year	4th year	5th year
	Total Capacity: leaf plates 6 lakh (assorted), leaf cups 10 lakh (assorted)						
	Sales revenue		16.1	20.16	24.66	26.64	28.08
B.	Cost of production per annum						
B1	Raw Materials*		1.5	1.6	1.7	1.8	1.9
B2	Cost of utilities		0.36	0.36	0.36	0.36	0.36
B3	Manpower		7.2	7.5	7.8	8.1	8.4
B4	Office & Marketing expenses		4.2	4.44	4.68	4.92	5.16
	Total of Cost of Production		13.26	13.9	14.54	15.18	15.82
C	Net Profit (before tax)		2.84	6.26	10.12	11.46	12.26

BREAK EVEN POINT ANALYSIS

Break-even point

$$\frac{Annual\ Fixed\ Cost \times 100}{Annual\ Fixed\ Cost + Profit} = \%$$

Sl. No.	Particulars	Year 1	Year 2	Year 3	Year 4	Year 5
	Gross Sales	16.1	20.16	24.66	26.64	28.08
A1	Less: Work in progress goods	-	1.6	2.1	2.5	2.9
A2	Add: Closing Stock	1.6	2.1	2.5	2.9	3.1
A	Total Sale	17.7	20.66	25.06	27.04	28.28
	Variable & Semi variable expenses					
B1	Raw Materials	1.5	1.6	1.7	1.8	1.9
B2	Power (85%)	0.306	0.306	0.306	0.306	0.306
B3	Manpower (60%)	4.32	4.50	4.68	4.86	5.04
B4	Admin & Marketing expenses (80%)	3.36	3.552	3.744	3.936	4.128
B5	Interest on WC loan	0.35	0.35	0.35	0.35	0.35
B6	Repairs and maintenance	0.20	0.20	0.20	0.20	0.20
B	Total Variable & Semi variable expenses	10.036	10.508	10.98	11.452	11.924
	Contribution (A-B)	7.664	10.152	14.08	15.588	16.356
	Fixed & Semi-fixed expenses					
C1	Power (15%)	0.054	0.054	0.054	0.054	0.054
C2	Manpower (40%)	2.88	3.00	3.12	3.24	3.36
C3	Depreciation @10%	0.25	0.25	0.25	0.25	0.25
C4	Admin & Marketing expenses (20%)	0.84	0.888	0.936	0.984	1.032
C5	Rent	1.20	1.20	1.20	1.20	1.20
C	**Total Fixed & Semi-fixed expenses**	5.224	5.392	5.56	5.728	5.896
C	Operating Profit (B-C)	2.44	4.76	8.52	9.86	10.46
	Break Even Point (%)	68	53	40	37	36

References

- **Entrepreneurindia.co Reports on BANANA LEAVES Plates**

- **Report on Leaf on cups plates by TIMEIS**

- **Niir Project Consultancy Services on Banana Leaf Plate Manufacturing**

  Video Link – Ready to Use and throw utensils

  https://youtu.be/aLyUsVnllHE

MANUFACTURES/ SUPPLIERS OF MACHINERY

- Shree Murugan Industries, Plot No. 68/W, Hootagalli, Industrial Area Belawadi Post, Mysore – 571186

- AMI Eng. Station Road, Opposite Veena Cinema, Patna - 800 001

- Chandan Eng Works, Industrial Estate, Kurji Patna - 800 010, Kalpataru Enterprises, HIG, Sector E, Aliganj Scheme, Lucknow - 226 020

- Nalanda Agro Works, Nalanda Nagar, Kurji Patna- 800 010

- Anil & Co. 68, NGO's Colony, Rajendra Nagar, Mysore - 570 007

STATUTORY/ GOVERNMENT APPROVALS

- Obtain the GST registration.
- Additionally, obtain the Udyog Aadhar registration Number.
- IEC Code for Export of end products and local authority clearance may be required for Shops and Establishment.
- Obtain ESI, PF and Labour laws may be required if applicable
- Fire Registration as required.
- Choice of a Brand Name of the product and secure the name with Trademark if required

DISCLAIMER:

This is an indicative illustration of project profile; the above calculation can vary with the locations. Only few machine manufacturers are mentioned in the profile, although many machine manufacturers are available in the market. The addresses given for machinery manufacturers have been taken from reliable sources, to the best of knowledge and contacts. However, no responsibility is admitted, in case any inadvertent error or incorrectness is noticed therein. Further, the same have been given by way of information only and do not carry any recommendation.

Refernce

1. Government of India MSME portal
2. SIDBI Portal
3. Various journals downloaded from Internet
4. Books of Indian Institute of Banking & Finance
5. Publications and handbooks
   from ministry of MSME
1. Language correction & spelling correction
   support taken in copilot